GROW
MARIJUANA
NOW!

GROW MARIJUANA NOW!

Includes information about CULTIVATING WEED INDOORS and OUTDOORS

AN INTRODUCTORY, STEP-BY-STEP GUIDE TO GROWING CANNABIS

Alicia Williamson

Avon, Massachusetts

Published by
Adams Media, a division of F+W Media, Inc.
57 Littlefield Street, Avon, MA 02322. U.S.A.
www.adamsmedia.com

Contains material adapted and abridged from *The Everything® Marijuana Book*
by Alicia Williamson, copyright © 2009 by F+W Media, Inc.,
ISBN 10: 1-4405-0687-6, ISBN 13: 978-1-4405-0687-1.

ISBN 10: 1-4405-1091-1
ISBN 13: 978-1-4405-1091-5
eISBN 10: 1-4405-1092-X
eISBN 13: 978-1-4405-1092-2

Printed in the United States of America.

10 9 8 7 6 5 4 3 2 1

Library of Congress Cataloging-in-Publication Data
is available from the publisher.

Interior illustrations by Eric Andrews.

This book is available at quantity discounts for bulk purchases.
For information, please call 1-800-289-0963.

ACKNOWLEDGMENTS

I would like to acknowledge the contributions to this book of Dr. Richard Bayer, MD, particularly his medical cannabis expertise and his wonderful capsule research and recipe.

I would also like to acknowledge Robert Connell Clarke. I first received a copy of his *Marijuana Botany* in 1981. It opened up my eyes to the world of cannabis breeding in an entirely new and exciting way, and for that I am very grateful.

And, finally, I would like to thank my dear husband, Richard Volkman, for doing all the farm chores for the last three months and making me grilled cheese sandwiches to eat in front of my computer while I wrote.

CONTENTS

CHAPTER ONE

GETTING STARTED

This book is about growing marijuana—not the politics of marijuana; the legality (or illegality) of its possession, use, or sale; the beneficial medical effects of marijuana; the history of marijuana; nor the economics of marijuana. While all of these topics may be related to your decision to grow and consume marijuana—and might make for interesting reading—they will not be covered here. Except for those instances when background information directly assists the reader in selecting particular methods or making practical cultivation decisions, this book is about growing marijuana. Only. It is designed to provide the beginner all the information necessary to grow marijuana quickly, successfully, and economically.

There are plenty of considerations, options, and choices available for both the casual and serious marijuana grower. In the following pages, you'll find the major—and minor—issues explained so that you will be able to successfully fit cannabis cultivation into your situation and lifestyle.

Economic and Time Considerations

Because economics are a big consideration, this book will help you make rational decisions by pointing out what kind of investment yields what kind of result. While it's possible to spend big bucks in this endeavor, it's not necessary. You don't want to bankrupt yourself, and this book should help prevent that. You can also spend a lot of time on this process, depending how deeply you get into it. For most people, growing marijuana is a hobby or pastime and not an occupation, so it's important to know what needs to be done and be able to do it quickly.

For that reason, you'll find two kinds of special hints throughout this book. The first is the "Low-Cost Tip," which will guide you in the most economical methods of growing marijuana. The second is the "Hassle-Free Tip," which is designed to reduce the effort involved. These tips outline the basic, minimal steps necessary to grow weed.

Commitment

Growing cannabis requires an investment of time, effort, and money. This book is designed to help you get the greatest from your investment by explaining the most cost- and time-effective methods of doing things. And there are lots and lots of things to do when growing cannabis.

Yes, you could just throw some seeds in the ground and let nature take its course, but the chances that this technique will achieve satisfactory results are close to nil. Instead, you should be prepared to make a plan and follow it faithfully. Taking care of living plants, which need the proper amount of light, nourishment, and protection from disease, insects, and predation (in animal and human form), will require a commitment on your part. They're just plants, but they're *your* plants. You will need to achieve a level of responsibility for your garden in order to make your effort worthwhile.

Decisions, Decisions

Before you run out to stock up on rolling papers, you'll need to make some decisions on how to go about this adventure. Some of these decisions may be simple, or already made for you by your circumstances—others may require significant planning. Following is a list of the major choices involved in starting and maintaining a marijuana crop.

- **Indoors or out.** This question will depend on your climate, whether suitable space is available either indoors or out, and how you will provide security for your grow.
- **Seeds or cuttings.** What are your sources? While obtaining seeds from a reputable vendor is your best bet, you may want to try some seed you've been saving or source cuttings.
- **Quantity.** Do you want to grow enough for yourself and a friend or two, or do you have commerce in mind?
- **Grow for seeds or just for smoke?** The easiest way is to buy seeds every time you want to plant a new crop. But if you want to eliminate that expense, or if you just wish to be self-sufficient, you can propagate—breed new plants—by fertilization for seeds or by cloning. Read Chapter 5: Propagation to understand what's involved. You may want to experiment, you may feel this

aspect of gardening is fun, or you may find that you have no interest in the process.

- **Budget.** Depending on the size of your grow, you could be looking at serious money. An indoor grower will need soil, fertilizer, lights, fans, filters, and a lot of electricity to operate all those devices. An outdoor grower will spend less but will still have expenses to deal with.
- **Security issues.** There are different ways to ensure you are not caught by authorities and not discovered by thieves.
- **Recordkeeping.** The more serious you are, the greater the importance of keeping accurate records. But it's up to you.

What You Need to Know

All of the issues in the preceding list are covered in thorough detail in the following pages. You may want to read through the entire book for the big-picture view before taking any actions and buying your materials. Or if you have a pretty good idea already that you are growing indoors, you can skip Chapters 9 and 10; outdoor growers can skip Chapters 7 and 8.

CHAPTER TWO

INDOORS VERSUS OUTDOORS

Probably the most important part of this equation is considering what the plants will need. The other part to consider is what you need and actually want to do. A small outdoor grow takes about the same effort as a small, personal-use vegetable garden. If your goal is only a few ounces for the year, a tiny container garden on your deck might suffice. If you are supplying medical cannabis patients, you will need to evaluate their needs and compare those needs to how much you can realistically expect to produce for them.

Climate Considerations

The first thing to think about is where you live. Your geographic location determines your climate and seasonal growing conditions. These factors will impact how well different strains of cannabis will grow outdoors. Of course, if you are planning on indoor growing, you can dictate climate conditions and manipulate light, thus controlling where the plants think they are growing. This control gives the indoor grower more choice as to different strains. Bear in mind that the indoor grower must also balance her choices, as each strain will not have an individual vegetative or flowering room; they will have to keep to a medium range that is acceptable to all the strains growing together.

It is not advisable to have only one strain growing at a time. The risk of a complete crop failure increases as the genetic similarity of the plants will tend to make them uniformly susceptible. If a particular strain is, for example, found to be mold prone, you could lose your whole crop. If your crop has genetic diversity, there is a far greater chance that some strains will be resistant to whatever plague might choose to visit you. Also, if you harvest a crop of genetically identical plants, you will get easily bored using exactly the same cannabis day in and day out; variety is far preferred.

Also, another factor to consider about your climate is many states have punitive laws about growing cannabis; you are well advised to educate yourself as to the statutes in your locality.

If you are lucky, you live in a medical cannabis state and can obtain legal permissions, at least on the state level. Otherwise, with very few exceptions, almost every state's laws consider growing or manufacturing recreational cannabis (even small amounts for your own personal use) to be a felony.

Only you can assess the risk you are willing to take, but checking the laws in your state might be helpful in understanding and evaluating that risk. Go to the website of the National Organization for the Reform of Marijuana Laws (NORML) at *www.norml.org* and select your state to see an up-to-date list of laws and penalties. Very few people realize how serious law enforcement can be about what is, after all, only a plant.

Medical Cannabis States

Do you live in a state that currently has medical cannabis laws? Although cannabis remains illegal, and a Schedule I drug under United States federal law, many (currently fourteen) states have passed medical marijuana laws.

States that have legalized medical marijuana

Since 1996, the states that have passed medical marijuana laws are: Alaska, California, Colorado, Hawaii, Maine, Michigan, Montana, Nevada, New Jersey, New Mexico, Oregon, Rhode Island, Vermont, and Washington.

In almost all of these states, patients are required to produce their own cannabis, or to designate an individual to produce it for them. Some states have dispensary programs, but mostly patients are on their own and, like most recreational users, must turn to the black market if they lack a grower.

Another real benefit of living in a medical cannabis state is your increased access to different strains and to helpful knowledge. Medical cannabis patients can network openly, and, depending upon their state's particular statute, can usually freely exchange medicine and plants.

If you are lucky enough to live in a state that has a medical marijuana law, it is imperative, as a prospective grower, to do your research. It is extremely foolish to ignore statutes that, if followed, will provide you with very real protection from state and local law enforcement agencies.

City, Suburb, Rural?

City and suburban growers are mostly forced to grow indoors; otherwise, they will usually raise plants for cannabis thieves, commonly known as "rippers." This name is particularly apt, as not only are they ripping you off, but also the smash and grab tactics commonly used involve literally ripping the plants from the earth or apart.

The last thing you want is to have strangers targeting your home and your plants. With that warning in mind, however, a smaller amount of cannabis plants can be intermixed with a regular garden and will frequently escape detection. Aerial searchers are also more prone to look in rural areas for bigger grows, while the suburban or city grower is more likely to be overlooked by taller buildings, or to have someone smell their plants. Rooftop grows are also becoming more common; they are usually far more secure than growing on a deck or in a backyard.

Rural grow sites have the advantage for outdoor growing. Many grows are discovered by passersby smelling the cannabis and doing a little investigating; acreage and proper placement of the crop eliminate this danger. Intermixing the cannabis with a summer vegetable garden will help keep the plants from aerial spotting. In the country, deer and livestock predations make high fencing common for noncannabis gardens, so casual observers would have no reason to suspect a cannabis crop is also being grown.

How Much Do You Want to Grow?

The second item to consider is how much you want to grow. Usually, the quick answer is: as much as possible! There are two kinds of answers to this question, as it can be taken in two different ways.

Growing Like a Gardener

One, how much do you *want* to grow? Do you already garden and think, "I can grow a great tomato plant, why would cannabis be any more difficult?" Do you look at friends' cannabis gardens and feel attracted to the plants themselves? If you answered yes, then you actually *want* to grow cannabis.

If you already feel like growing will be an added chore or boring labor, it is possible that you just do not have a feel for the enjoyment of gardening, no matter what you are growing. Or you might feel intimidated as to how difficult it might be. You could try growing a smallish amount and confirm that your real interest is in being a consumer, not a producer, of cannabis. Or, despite your initial reservations, you might find yourself captivated and fascinated and become a lifelong grower.

Growing for Supply

The other interpretation is how much do you want to grow? Is your purpose in growing to supply yourself or a friend or relative with medical cannabis? You need to sit down and figure out how many ounces a month are medically needed. Bear in mind that tinctures and medibles (edibles containing marijuana) use far more than ingestion by smoking.

As a first-time grower, make your calculations based on a yield of four to six ounces per plant. Once you know what you are doing, it is not unreasonable to expect a pound to a pound and a half per plant yields, but it is always better to be pleasantly surprised by a higher yield than to come up short.

If you plan to grow indoors at home, the sheer space limitations of your house may make your garden-size decision for you. It is not advisable to crowd indoor plants, as it will substantially reduce yields. Crowding, particularly during the flowering stage, also leads to problems with mold and mites. The space you use for your inside garden needs to be away from general family activities, and somewhere you can lock without appearing suspicious. Even if you are growing legally, there is no reason to (and many reasons not to) let anyone not directly concerned know about your grow.

You also have to think about home security. Placing the plants inside your home can keep them safer from thieves, but the downside is that inside plants put you at greater risk for a personal confrontation with a criminal or criminals.

You must also factor in the legal restrictions on plant numbers that pertain to your particular state. Also, some states limit the number of patients for whom a grower can legally grow. This number is important to know and abide by, as unpleasant interactions with law enforcement can literally ruin your life.

Keeping the Plants Healthy

Bear in mind the space requirements that large, healthy cannabis plants will need, especially outdoors. With a little effort on your part, these girls will get rather big; figure on at least six feet in height for sativas and, depending on your climate, possibly considerably more. Indicas tend to be shorter and bushier. Planting too closely can lead to poor air circulation and mold, so figure to give each female plant at least six feet in diameter space. Smaller plantings of low-growing herbs can be scattered in between; this makes it much harder to discern cannabis from the air.

The plants will need good sunlight, and lots of it. The plants will need water, and in quantities far greater than you will want to carry; there should be convenient access to good water. The plants will also need protection, mainly from other humans. Ideally the grow site will be where you can easily monitor day and night; this usually means near your house, unless you plan to sleep outside for the last month before harvest.

The other thing to consider in location is the actual distance from your house to the crop. This can be a factor if you are robbed and file a claim with your homeowner's insurance. It is worth checking your policy, as it has become more common for insurance to pay damages to legal medical cannabis growers when their plants are stolen. Sometimes there are restrictions on how far insured items can be from your actual house: something on the back forty, even though still on your property, probably would not be covered.

Indoor plants are usually grown in more crowded conditions, especially during their vegetative stage, but investing in fans for good air circulation and dehumidifers for moisture control will help keep the plants from molding. And with the ability to control their growth by controlling light, you can have shorter plants as well as a much shorter grow cycle than required for an outdoor crop.

Budget Considerations

One very important factor to consider as you plan: what kind of budget are you working with?

Indoor Costs

Indoor growing can be particularly hard on the pockets. A small indoor grow can run to $400 per month very easily, and that is just for ongoing electricity costs. The initial purchase of building materials for vegetative and flowering rooms (each of which requires a different light cycle and different lights), fans, dehumidifiers, filters, ballasts, grow lights, and the bulbs (which wear out and need replacing), containers, and soil can be prohibitive. Other ongoing expenses include renewing the soil mixture for each crop, different mineral additives, and water bills.

HASSLE-FREE TIP

Both indoor and outdoor grows are safer with security systems. Your budget will decide whether you go with a large dog or an expensive and sophisticated alarmed motion system. Once installed, however, a carefully considered system will prevent a lot of anxiety.

Outdoor Costs

Outdoor growing has the advantage of using the sun for free. Other than that bonus from nature, you must factor in the start-up costs of fencing, improving your soil, water, mineral additives, and a drying area for after the harvest.

Fencing needs to be high and of stout materials. It has three functions: to screen your garden from casual observers, to keep out livestock and wild browsers like deer, and to keep out rippers. For optimizing ripper protection, use a high boarded fence to minimize visibility, electric wire on the inside of the fence top to discourage climbers, and heavy gauge wire or stock panels around the plants.

Soil improvement can involve digging out compacted clay soils and replacing with your own compost and a sandy loam mix, or replacing with expensive, bagged organic soils. It all depends on the initial condition of your site's soil. The more years you use a site, the better your soil will become, but it will always need mulches, new compost, and minerals each time you renew your garden.

Outdoor Money-Saving Ideas

If expenses are a major concern, plan ahead and improve your soil by mulching and composting with free materials. Leaves are everywhere in the fall and are an excellent choice for improving soil. Mulch your areas in the fall and till in the composted leaves in the spring. Rain-spoiled hay is usually available for free or very cheaply in the country and is an excellent mulch.

When drying the crop, consider the expense for a dedicated building or drying room, purchasing fans and dehumidifiers, and the accompanying electrical bills to power them.

The Co-Op Advantage

Another possibility for a first-time grower is to think about a cooperative grow. This provides an opportunity to share information and strains, as well as expenses and space. If you can join a cooperative with a master grower already in place, you can learn in a hands-on environment.

Growing cannabis in a cooperative is also a great low-cost option, particularly for the new grower. If one grower has the land, others can provide labor and supplies, or share in costs for water, minerals, and other costs of production.

Another benefit is in sharing the security duties; you may not enjoy being constantly tied to your crop until harvest. A partner or partners in a crop can help each other and, of course, help with the harvesting and cleaning of the final crop.

Choosing the Right Strains

Once you have decided where to grow (indoors, outdoors, or a mixture of both), what strains of cannabis will give you the optimum chance of success? Cannabis breeders have spent years modifying plant characteristics, so where the strains are typically grown can give you your first clue as to what might optimize your growing success.

Indoor

Generally, indoor plants that have been hybridized for that purpose have had the height bred out of them; the goal is short, productive, mold- and pest-resistant plants. The grower has the option of starting the flowering cycle by light trigger and limiting vegetative growth, but the overall form and lankiness of pure sativas do not lend themselves well to indoor grows. Pure indicas or sativa/indica hybrids will generally perform much better and lead to happier results for the grower.

Most new growers are better off starting small. Growing cannabis is an expensive proposition, whether indoors or outdoors, and it is best to start out slowly and see if you really have the time and money required. Experience whether you enjoy or dislike the process, and test out how viable and secure your envisioned grow site truly is.

Indica type. Note the rounded chubby leaves and stocky nature of the plant.

If nothing else, your experiments in growing will make you a wiser and better consumer, with more understanding of how and why one grower's cannabis is better than another's. There is no shame in deciding that you are not cut out to be a grower; appreciative consumers are always needed for any product and are, in return, appreciated by the grower who grows for the love of it.

Outdoor

Outdoor plants need an environment that matches their genetic predisposition. For example, a hybrid cross that introduces an indica, like the classic Northern Lights, will do much better somewhere like the Pacific Northwest. This is where the importance of provenance and knowing the growing characteristics of a strain (its finish, typical plant structure, and mold resistance) are extremely helpful.

It is interesting to note that the same strain, started indoors and then moved to an outside grow, will look very different from the original mother plant grown from seed outdoors. This is an example of how the genotype expresses differently in different environments and how early the adaptation starts. A plant started indoors and then transplanted outdoors usually grows very bush-like, while the 100 percent outdoor-grown plant will have a more treelike appearance with a thick trunk and

Sativa type. Note the rangy structure and narrow leaves.

longer axials. Due to the outdoor cycle's long growing period, and chances of rain soaking the plant near harvest time, the treelike structure is more suited to an outdoor grow. Its air circulation is better than a super bushy, dense structure that is more prone to molds if the leaves get watered. The indoor grower has less concern as she can control where she waters.

CHAPTER THREE
GROWING FROM SEEDS OR CLONES

An individual cannabis plant has its own genetically determined unique characteristics, or genotype. The grower propagates selectively in order to replicate desirable characteristics; in the cannabis plant these can include psychoactive effect, medical effect, aroma, taste, size, and flower type. The genotype can be influenced environmentally and ultimately expressed visibly in what is called the phenotype. This can be seen by growing two genetically identical plants under different conditions. One grown in shade might appear very long and tall, compared to its clone grown in full sunlight that matures as a more compact, bushy looking plant. To ensure a successful result, start with the best individuals you can procure, and provide the correct environment.

Clones or Seedlings

The question of how to start your marijuana garden may be answered for you. Most people have saved some seeds—often for many years—for just this occasion. There are several negatives to using seeds, but you can use them without involving anyone else, and the price is right. If you decide to use clones, you'll need to find a supplier.

Clones

Clones, or rooted cuttings from a female or mother plant, have many advantages. The genotype is a known entity. The grower knows already that the clone is female and that the plant possesses characteristics of value to the grower. There is no need to wait for the young plant to display sexual differentiation; it can go immediately into a fast-track growing mode. This is particularly helpful when the outdoor grower has a short growing season, as it sidesteps the waiting time for sexual differentiation needed for seed-propagated starts.

If the grower is providing medical cannabis to patients, it is important to remember that clones are very valuable in assuring that the patients get strains that actually help with their medical condition(s). Most medical cannabis patients have experimented with different strains until they found the ones that work best for their condition; genetic uniformity is essential if the grower is to supply cannabis as medicine.

Seedlings

Seedlings come from seed. Seed propagation also has advantages. If stored properly, cannabis seed remains viable for years. Unlike a clone, which immediately needs soil, light, water, and care, the seed will wait for you. This is a convenience, even if you plan to just buy seed and not breed on your own. Seed is also a way for a breeder to easily bank certain genetics that he might want to reintroduce at a later point in developing a strain. Trying to store genetics by repeatedly cloning is time-consuming and takes up far more space.

All seed is created by sexual propagation. Cannabis makes this interesting for the breeder as it is a *dioecious* plant, requiring both a male and a female plant to produce viable seed. Sometimes cannabis will produce hermaphrodites. This is an undesirable characteristic, and these individuals should be destroyed. Hermaphrodites can pollinate themselves and the rest of your crop if you let them.

Many growers produce crops that are a combination of both clones and seedlings. The clones provide the completely known entities, while the seedlings are an opportunity to produce a genetic sport, something new, in an aim to improve one or more characteristics supplied by the parent plants.

Seed is more versatile than taking clones; you can select plants for specific desirable traits and produce your own individualized hybrid strains. Instead of relying on other breeders, you have more independence from outside sources and can control the genetic direction of the breeding program.

A seedling also has the potential to be a male plant, needed for pollen, and, depending on the growing trends in one's area, perhaps rather rare. Many growers who work exclusively with clones instead of seed are horrified by male plants, viewing them as a threat to the production of seedless, or sinsemilla, high-grade cannabis. Despite exaggerated fears of out-of-control pollination, a home grower can easily ensure that a male plant is isolated and only used for controlled pollination and fertilization of specific females. To a seed breeder, males, particularly from a prized strain, are very valuable in their own right because without males there is no advancement of the strain.

Which Is Easier, Clone or Seedling?

The first-time grower should not feel intimidated by the idea of growing from seed, but your first grow will be less complicated if you start out with clones. You can leapfrog over seed germination and move right to planting.

> ### HASSLE-FREE TIP
> Think of clones like going to the garden center and buying a healthy young tomato plant instead of a packet of seed. With reasonable care, all of your clones will grow to be healthy plants without needing germination.

Also, with clones, your plant count will stay mostly the same from start to finish (barring pests, rippers, and accidental breakage to young clones), the plants will be more or less what you expected as far as genotype, and there will be no anxiety about accurately sexing the young plants. And, having females, you still have the option of procuring pollen from another grower and breeding some seeds for next season.

Growing from Clones

Let's start with beginning a garden of clones. Assuming you have organized and prepared your garden area, indoor or outdoor, your first question is probably: Where can I get clones? If you live in a medical cannabis state, there is a good possibility that clones or cuttings are available from a local compassion organization or from meetings where patients and their caregivers/growers gather to share concerns and cannabis. This is an opportunity to sample various strains and identify which types of cannabis are locally available.

Many meetings have clone tables where growers can acquire labeled strains for free or a nominal fee or donation. Be sure to discuss the characteristics of the clones you select; not only their effects, but find out what the propagator has observed as far as their performance during the growing phase. Ideally, of course, you will already know a grower who will take cuttings and make rooted clones of various strains that you specify.

Note that sometimes you will receive cuttings from a mother plant that have not yet produced roots and made the transition to being a real plant. These will require a little more attention than rooted clones, and you should expect a little more attrition; not all cuttings are going to root. If you are in the position where you have to get cuttings to root, always start with more than you think you are going to need.

A complete explanation of handling and planting a clone is provided in "How to Take a Cutting" and "Rooting a Cutting" in Chapter 5: Propagation. The techniques and materials are the same whether you obtain cuttings from others or take the cuttings yourself.

Recordkeeping

Be careful to get as much information as possible on the genetic origins of the strains: accurate information will be very useful to you as you raise the plant. If you plan to breed the plant, knowing something about the parents can help you decide which males will be the most likely to add the characteristics to improve performance.

Be aware that there are casual, if not dishonest, people who will misrepresent their clone as being a certain popular strain. Until you have a trusted source for cuttings or clones, or have started breeding or cloning your own plants, always note the name of the strain with a bit of skepticism. The same applies to casually acquired seeds; they may or may not be what is reported.

This does not necessarily mean that people are deliberately lying to you; it is just that people forget, or information gets translated incorrectly from person to person. Of course, this low-key attitude toward sketchy information only applies to free, as in freely given, seed or clones.

If you are going to buy clones or seed, either know the grower or buy from a well-established seed bank. A reputable high-end seed bank will absolutely guarantee their breeding program and seed provenance beyond question.

What Type?

Cannabis can express itself very differently from strain to strain and even plant to plant.

Knowing the characteristics of the parents will also help you know if you have an outdoor strain or an indoor strain—or one that seems comfortable and obliging no matter where you grow it. A sativa bred to be sixteen feet tall outdoors is going to have a miserable time growing in a low-ceilinged basement grow room where a chubby little indica type will be much more productive and easier to handle. A late-finishing strain may not do as well in an outdoor grow, especially if your season is short. If you are growing it indoors, you can easily manipulate the same strain's finish time by controlling the timing of the light it receives, but you will save yourself some frustration if you have accurate information.

Be very careful to label the clone with strain and date, and write down any other information you've acquired in your grow book (see Chapter 14: Recordkeeping). You may think you will remember everything at a later date, but you might miss important details and information. You will be using this information some years down the road if you continue as a cannabis grower. Good recordkeeping is essential, not only for your own needs, but for the credibility of your strains' provenance. To serious growers, correct identification of a plant's genetics is essential; the effort and expense of growing high-grade cannabis precludes operating from guesswork. The plant should be labeled from cutting to clone to plant and to hanging, drying plant; in other words, at *all times.*

HASSLE-FREE TIP

A plastic label marked with indelible pen should be either stuck in the soil at the base of the plant or affixed with a twist tie to an axial branch. This way, you'll always know what you are dealing with.

Growing from Seeds

Perhaps clones are not available to you, or you just like the idea of growing your plants from seeds. Many people have small bags of seeds they've kept over the years, possibly labeled, probably not. If these are your only option, it is not the worst thing in the world; you kept those seeds for a reason, most likely because you enjoyed the cannabis it came from (though you might have cursed at the time if you spent good money for sinsemilla, or seedless, cannabis).

If you are on a tight budget, have no seeds of your own, and are shocked by commercially produced seed prices, perhaps a nongrowing friend has some seeds. If your friend generally consumes what you consider to be high-end cannabis, he may contribute something rather special. Growers call these sorts of seeds "randoms" or sometimes "unknown soldiers." This is somewhat akin to buying a surprise package or an abandoned storage locker at auction; you have no real idea of what you will get, but sometimes you end up with something very nice.

HASSLE-FREE TIP

While expensive, mail order seeds generally are very good quality and of known provenance. Most seeds come from Amsterdam or Canada. If you are especially fond of a popular commercial strain, you can generally acquire it by mail order.

Ideally, however, you will get your seeds from a known source, a breeder or grower you know personally or a trusted mail order house in Canada or Amsterdam. If you plan to grow outdoors, locally bred seed from outdoor plants has the advantage of already being acclimated to your home growing conditions.

Feminized Seed

Some mail order strains are feminized, or guaranteed to be female plants. Feminized cannabis seeds start with selected female clones that are manipulated environmentally to produce male flowers and pollen and bred back to themselves. Feminized seeds are difficult to produce but are purported to deliver all (99 percent) female plants. Feminized seeds also are believed to produce genetically stable plants, which is useful in a breeding program; however, some growers report hermaphrodism as a problem. If you plan to use feminized seeds, it is better to purchase them from a reputable seed bank, as most will guarantee that the seed will produce females.

Seed Storage

To keep seeds viable, store them in a dry, dark, cool place and in dry, airtight glass containers. Make certain they are clearly labeled with their source and the year of production. Although it is advisable to use fresh seed when possible, cannabis seeds are very strong and long lasting.

Although definitely not the best practice because viability is affected by aging, growers have been known to germinate seeds as old as twenty years, if not older. Ideally, you will use the seed within three years of production. As the seed ages, a smaller proportion will germinate successfully.

Growers germinate very old seed (as in twenty-plus years) out of interest, just for fun, and sometimes because they have no other choice. One grower reported amazement at the nostalgic recognition and feeling of reuniting with the long-ago plant via its daughter.

As noted, using old seed is not a best practice, but it is sometimes useful if a hybrid strain starts manifesting unwanted characteristics. The breeder can go back a few generations and rework the strain forward by introducing desired characteristics from another line. It is also comforting to know that you, as the breeder, can revisit a particularly good year by germinating and propagating the siblings of superior plants.

Selecting Seeds

Unless you have paid big dollars for feminized seed, plan on starting twice as many seeds as the final number of female plants you hope to raise to fruition. The ratio of males to females is generally 1:1. Of course, you are dealing with living entities, so this will vary.

Examine your seeds carefully under magnification; a jeweler's loupe or handheld magnifying glass will work fine. Remove and dispose of any seeds that are cracked or have holes. Check for the most mature seeds. Depending on the strains you are working with, the mature seeds will be either very dark brown with lighter brown striping, or a strong green-gray with brown striping. Pale whitish green seed with no striping are immature and should be discarded.

Germinating Seed

Seeds require moisture, warmth, and darkness for successful germination. Before you start soaking your seeds, you need to plan ahead so that you can consistently provide all three. To prepare your seed soaking area, assess how well it meets germination requirements; the area should be dark and warm, 65°F–80°F, ideally 70°F. Some growers use seed-starting mats that maintain an ideal temperature, but a warm closet or kitchen cupboard (on an inside wall) will usually be fine.

HASSLE-FREE TIP

An infrared laser surface thermometer is an invaluable and inexpensive tool. These are sold for cooks, but they take a lot of worry out of seed starting. You can check temperature instantly and take steps to correct an environment that is too cold or too warm.

A foil-covered cookie sheet makes a good tray for small bowls or jars. If you are starting different strains, make certain your labels are prepared and affixed to each tray or bowl so you can keep track of which seed is which strain. You will need a convenient light source as you will be checking the seeds frequently for germination, as well as monitoring moisture. You do not want the seeds to dry out.

Some growers use plastic zip-top bags filled with clean water for germination. These have an advantage as you can turn the bag and examine the seeds for activity without actually touching the seeds. Also, since they are sealed, less water is lost to evaporation, and it protects against having your seeds dry out. On the other hand, the bags make it more difficult to remove and plant a seed that

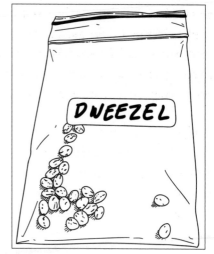

Labeled plastic bag with seeds.

has cracked and shown a tiny white root tip (usually referred to as having "tailed") since all the seed will not tail at once.

Many growers use small water glasses or jam jars and float the seeds in clean water. Others use small shallow bowls with squares of paper towel cut to fit. The seeds sit on moistened paper towels and are covered by a thin layer of damp towels on top. The top layer is easily lifted to check the seeds. The paper towel method mimics nature more closely (simulating the damp soil a seed would have fallen to) and is the easiest for removing germinated seeds for planting.

Remember, at this point you will have started your grow book and will note the date you start soaking your seeds. Fresh seeds generally tail within twenty-four to forty-eight hours, but some, particularly older seeds, can take up to a week or even ten days.

Check your seeds twice a day, but avoid handling them excessively. You are looking for germination, but also stay on top of moisture requirements. Do not let the seeds dry out; this almost always kills the seed embryo. If you are using the small bowl method, a chopstick is useful for gently turning or separating seeds from each other so you can look for the tiny white tail. As soon as a seed tails, note the date in your book. This is part of the history of this particular plant.

Preparing to Plant

While you are waiting for your seeds to germinate, you can prepare your first little seedling pots. You will need 4-inch plastic pots, new and clean, or previously used ones carefully washed with a light bleach solution and then rinsed with clean water. These can be set up on trays and ready to label. An indelible pen can be used to write directly onto the pots, or some growers use a garden center plastic stick for the information and just move the stick with the plant as it gets transplanted to bigger containers.

Seed planting will go easier if you have a clear, clean, well-lighted work area, and you assemble your materials ahead of time. Germinated seeds are fragile, so plan your time so you can work without hurrying.

The soil mix for seedlings should be light, clump free, and well drained. Seeds need moisture, but excessive soil wetness can lead to a condition called damp-off where the little taproot becomes infected with a fungus parasite and rots. Once this happens, you lose the seedling. To prevent this from happening, start with sterilized soil, avoid heavy watering, and provide adequate ventilation.

As soon as the little seed tails, it needs to be planted. Do not wait; this is why you are checking the seeds at least twice a day. Leaving a germinated seed floating in water will kill it and you will have wasted your time and your seed.

Planting the Seed

You will need:

- Sterilized potting soil
- Clean 4-inch pots
- A chopstick or pencil marked to ½-inch from tip
- A clean mister bottle with clean water
- Sharpie or other indelible pen

Use a chopstick or pencil that you have measured off and marked a half-inch above the tip for making a "drill" (as a seed hole is known). Make sure the potting soil is uniformly damp (if the soil is dry when you fill your pots, give it a good soak, stir with the ever-useful chopstick to make certain there are no dry spots, soak again, and let drain). Make a half-inch drill into the soil in the center of each pot, and you are ready to plant some seeds.

Using thumb and forefinger, very gently grasp the seed at the opposite end from its tail. Place the seed in the mouth of the drill, tail down. This is the taproot, so heading the right direction is helpful to the seedling. Seeds that are planted upside down will eventually find their way and turn, but it takes time and is less than ideal for the plant.

Once the seed is in the drill, gently cover it with damp potting soil, and water the drill lightly with a teaspoonful of clean water. Note the planting date in your grow book.

Locating the Pots

Place your trays of pots in a warm, humid environment, 67°F–78°F, and keep moist but not soaking wet. A mister bottle with clean water is the best way to add moisture to your seedling pots. If you are starting plants or planning on growing indoors, use horticultural lights or a south-facing, well-lighted window bay. At this point, a small fan will provide adequate air circulation for the seed trays; the gently moving air will help prevent damp-off.

Use a thermometer to make certain that the germinating area is truly warm (67°F–78°F). Trying to germinate seed if it's too cold is a complete waste of seed and time. Now you will wait for your little seedlings to ideally push vigorously from the soil; this should occur within a day or so, but be patient. Do not over water, as this can drown your little start; just keep the soil lightly moist by using your mister bottle.

Hardening Off

Outdoor growers frequently start indoors under lights and transfer the seedlings after the last frost date for their area. The transfer from indoors to outdoors will require a short period of hardening off in a cold frame to minimize shock in young seedlings or clones.

Making a Cold Frame

Make a cold frame by placing an old window on top of a low cinderblock square. Three to four cinderblocks in height is sufficient. The window is easily propped for ventilation during warm days. To avoid chilling the plants, always have the open side opposite prevailing winds. Close the window on cold days, and at night cover with a blanket or some other type of insulation.

There are also some excellent and inexpensive heavy plastic greenhouses now available. An 8-by 8-foot greenhouse can be acquired for under $200, including some pea gravel for the floor.

Most have different zippered windows that can be adjusted for ventilation. These work very well for the hardening-off phase.

And, of course, if you are starting out with a small experiment in growing and do not want to make cold frames or buy greenhouses, it is perfectly viable to wait until all danger of frost is past. Then germinate your seed, plant in the starter pots, keep them moist, and set them in a secured area outside to pop up and start growing.

Seedlings in pots (approximately 3-inch to 4-inch plants).

CHAPTER FOUR

THE SOIL/GROWING MEDIUMS

The first-time grower may ask: "Why not just use premade potting soils and be done with it?" This is an option, albeit a rather expensive one, if you are growing more than a few plants on your deck. Raising healthy plants of any kind requires the grower to provide nutrients and to activate the microbial life in the soil. This is what feeds the plants.

What Is the Best Soil Mix for Cannabis?

Think about the nature of cannabis and what the plant needs for optimum growth and flowering. The final goal for the cannabis grower is large, healthy plants with large, healthy, resin-covered flowers. Without the proper soil mix and proper feeding during the grow, your plants could end up stunted, unproductive, and with inferior flowers.

Once your little seedlings are above ground, they are in a phase of vegetative growth. The plant is building healthy roots, making green leaves, and growing in size and height. The right mix at this time will make the difference between stunted, starved little plants and large, luscious, green, and happy plants. You need large roots to support a large superstructure.

Cannabis is a big feeder and fast grower. Many a novice grower has been astonished by transplanting off schedule or late and finding the container completely filled with a dense root ball. This is also why container growers must top feed on schedule: a plant in the ground can reach out and search for more food, but the container-bound plant depends on you to feed it.

The basic requirement of cannabis is for nutrient-rich, well-drained soil. A good starter mix is one-third sandy loam for drainage, one-third compost you have made, and one-third organic bagged soil.

HASSLE-FREE TIP

You could just start out with an organic bagged soil, like Fox-Farm Ocean Forest Potting Soil, as it contains sandy loam already and is an excellent mix for cannabis. It is very expensive, but it's the easiest way to go.

Using sandy loam is important not only for the drainage but also for a slightly firmer soil texture; cannabis is less than happy with the typical fluffy structure of many commercial bagged potting soils. Sandy loam can be purchased in bulk at garden centers and by the yard at "feed and fuels" in rural areas.

Soil Types

An indoor grower may access soil or compost they have outside, but the outdoor grower has to consider whether to plant young plants directly into the ground or in large containers. There are good reasons for both alternatives. Containers protect plant roots from burrowing rodents and allow the grower to control exactly what soil the plant has access to. Growing in the ground allows cannabis to show its ability to get extremely large. Ground-planted cannabis is able to spread out its roots and grow.

If you plan to grow your plants in the ground in existing soil, you will need to identify your soil type so that you can amend it for optimum cannabis production. The main types of soil are as follows:

Clay

Clay soil is typically composed of 60 percent clay, 20 percent silt, and 20 percent sand. The clay actually has quite a few nutrients for the plant but is a very fine particle that tends to compact, interfering with the oxygen supply that plant roots require to actually use the nutrients. This compaction also makes the soil like concrete, allowing water to run off the surface so it cannot get to your plants' roots.

Obviously, clay soil is a poor choice for growing almost anything, let alone cannabis. If you plan to plant in the ground, you must dig out the offending clay and replace with your own amended soil mix. The bigger the hole, the better, but two to three feet in diameter and three feet deep will accommodate an outdoor plant quite well.

Adobe

Adobe is the mother of all clay soils; dig it out and replace, or, rather than struggle with iron-hard adobe, accept that you will be using containers and adjust your growing plans. You can try to amend adobe soil, but it will take years and truckloads of compost materials.

Sandy

Sandy soil can be very difficult to correct; it is on the other end of the spectrum from clay, as it drains too well and the plant loses the nutrients as water carries them away. It is also very wasteful of water and makes it difficult to know how much water the plants are actually receiving. A typical sandy soil will be almost 70 percent sand. If you have sandy soil, start amending it immediately with organic materials, but plan on growing your cannabis in containers for the first few years. It takes a lot of work to adjust sandy soils, although with time, lots of organic material, and patience, it can be improved.

Loam

Loam is the Holy Grail of soils. It retains nutrients and water for access by the plants and is very easy to work with. Most growers do not wake up one morning and have loam, but good organic gardening practices can improve a reasonable soil until it becomes loam. Loam is made up of 40 percent sand, 40 percent silt, and 20 percent clay. In this mix, the plant can access the good nutrients in clay soil because there is sufficient air available. When you are mixing your own soil, strive to match the blend that makes loam so special for plants.

Alternative Mediums for Growing

The so-called "soilless" or artificial soil mixes are inexpensive and sterile growing mediums used by commercial growers, particularly the hydroponics folks. Generally, artificial soils are made from perlite, vermiculite, peat moss, sand, and other components like coconut coir and pumice. Since the artificial soil is just a medium, if you plan to use it, be aware that you will have to supply all the nutrients the plants will need.

Perlite and Vermiculite

Perlite and vermiculite are both widely used in the horticultural industry because they are sterile and free from diseases, provide aeration and drainage, have a fairly neutral pH, are both nontoxic, and are relatively inexpensive. Indoor growers use them extensively, and outdoor growers frequently use them to lighten a soil mix.

Peat Moss

Peat moss is formerly living sphagnum moss from bogs that has partially decomposed. As a soil amendment, peat moss breaks down too fast, compressing the soil and creating an unhealthy lack of air for plant roots. It can be useful when lightened with perlite, but the mining of peat moss is an environmentally unsound practice.

Scraping off the top layer of living sphagnum moss affects the habitat for many rare plants, insects, and birds. For this reason, the cannabis grower who is also a friend to the environment should consider the implications of using peat moss.

If you must use this artificial soil, be aware that peat moss is quite acidic; check the pH level by testing the runoff water and adjust as needed.

Is Your Soil Healthy?

Plant roots need air to access food as well as water. A dense, compacted soil like clay may have lots of nutrients, but they remain unavailable to the plant due to lack of air. Good aeration stimulates beneficial bacterial activity, allowing the plant to use more organic matter.

Compacted soil will also speed up moisture loss: in packed soils, water rises very rapidly to the surface and is lost through evaporation. This can get frustrating, especially when you are paying a large water bill.

Minerals are also essential for healthy growth in cannabis. Most chemical fertilizers only focus on measuring levels of nitrogen, phosphorus, potassium, and calcium; these primary elements are essential, but used in excess can result in deficiencies in other elements your plants will need.

Cannabis prefers a soil that is not too acid and not too alkaline; a pH of 6.5 is just about perfect. Some growers swear by a slightly lower pH; most estimate that the range for soil-grown cannabis is 6.5 to 7.5.

Acidic soil will lock up nutrients, making them unavailable to your plant for growth and flowering. Highly acidic soil also damages the soil balance by limiting the growth of beneficial soil organisms. This is why you do not plant your cannabis in pure compost; too high of an organic content can raise the acid level to the point where your plant cannot use the nutrients you provide. Highly alkaline soil can lead to salt accumulation and limit the roots' ability to take up water.

The soil for your cannabis should be organic and alive. Cannabis is a consumable, like a vegetable, that you will put into your body. If you use organic, live soil, you will see greatly improved plant health and also notice an increase in the quality of your end product.

Why Use Living Soil?

Living soil organisms decompose organic compounds, sequester nitrogen and other nutrients, and fix nitrogen from the atmosphere, making it available to the plants. Soil organisms also prey on crop pests. Soil organisms interact with one another, with plants, and with the soil. The combined result is a number of beneficial functions including nutrient cycling, moderated water flow, and pest control.

Soil organic matter is used for the energy and nutrients the plants need. Bacteria, fungi, and other soil dwellers transform and release nutrients for the plants to use. In living soil, the soil directly around plant roots is teeming with bacteria. These bacteria feed on sloughed-off plant cells and the proteins and sugars released by roots. The protozoa and beneficial nematodes that eat the bacteria are also concentrated near roots. Complex organic compounds, called *humus*, remain after the many soil organisms have used and transformed the original material. Humus is important for improving water- and nutrient-holding capacities.

This nutrient cycling and disease suppression is very complex and very much needed by your plants. It is far better to work with nature and encourage natural controls than to dump in chemical fertilizers that will eventually destroy your soil.

How Do You Encourage Living Soil?

Start with compost. Successful compost building must balance four ingredients: carbon, nitrogen, moisture, and oxygen. Leaves, straw, and cornstalks are high in carbon. Manures provide nitrogen. Ideally, use three parts carbon-rich materials like dead leaves, shredded newspaper, straw, or cornstalks to one part nitrogen-rich materials like fresh leaves, manures, vegetable peelings, or fresh grass clippings.

Your pile should be at least three cubic feet, if not larger. If you use a composter, inoculate the mix with soil, finished compost, or fresh manure. You want the pile to get hot and "cook" in the beginning. The heat will kill weed or grass seeds that may be in the manures. Turn the pile once a week and keep it moist. The compost is ready when it is cool and looks like moist chocolate cake. It should smell good, like fresh-turned earth.

Compost can take nine to twelve months to mature, so outdoor cannabis gardeners should build compost piles in the fall. Some growers build a new compost pile over each plant site each fall. Then, in the spring, they mix it into their soil, test to see what amendments, if any, are needed, and the planting sites are ready and refreshed.

Soil Testing

Every type of plant has a different perfect level of soil acidity/alkalinity that allows it to perform to optimum standard. Cannabis in general prefers soil to be just slightly acid at 6.5. This is about the same as a tomato plant. If you have a garden spot where you have successfully grown large and healthy tomatoes, it is probably going to be all right for your cannabis. Soil pH is measured on a scale from 1.0 to 14.0. A pH of 7.0 is pH neutral; pH below 7.0 is considered to be acidic; and pH higher than 7.0 is considered to be alkaline.

The pH level of your soil will determine how well your plants are able to absorb nutrients. If the pH level is out of the proper range, the growth rate of the plants will slow down or even stop. Your plants will become visibly stressed. It is worthwhile to purchase a meter or test kit; you can put your young cannabis plants into properly balanced soil from the start and avoid stressing or damaging the plants from too high or low pH levels.

HASSLE-FREE TIP
A pH meter is long lasting and gives more accurate results than other methods of measuring pH. They have probes and batteries that eventually will need to be replaced, so consider a one-time use pH test kit. If you continue growing, and are continually buying new test kits, a meter can be a good investment.

If you are using purchased, bagged, premixed soils, the nitrogen, phosphorus, and potassium (N-P-K for short) levels should be listed. If you are mixing your own soil, it is advisable to test your soil for N-P-K using a soil test kit. These are easy to use, and there are reliable kits that contain separate tests for pH, nitrogen, phosphorus, and potassium.

A soil test kit will contain materials for a certain number of tests before you have to buy another; some can be used to check pH, nitrogen, phosphorus, and potassium levels ten times. Once you have tested your soil, you will probably need to make some amendments; cannabis is extremely forgiving of less than perfect soil conditions, but your goal is to raise healthy, productive plants that produce delicious, resin-covered flowers. If the plants are struggling, you will fall short of this goal.

Soil Amendments

Different organic soil amendments are usually needed when you are starting a grow site. Unlike chemical fertilizers, organics rarely burn plants, but testing your soil and understanding the different properties of different organic amendments can help you choose wisely. (It will help your budget, too.) Packaged amendments generally list the big three of plant needs as follows: nitrogen (N), phosphorus (P), and potassium (K). Always check, as extremely high nitrogen can burn plants.

Nitrogen and Manures

The great value of manure is its extended availability of nitrogen, which is of particular value in readily leached sandy soils. Nutrient content and rate of availability can vary, depending mostly on manure source or type, how it's applied, and water content. Fresh manure worked in immediately after spreading will retain the most nitrogen.

The advantages of adding organic matter content, and disadvantages of possible weed seed, should be considered in using uncomposted manure. Manures should be composted before using in direct contact with growing cannabis plants. Uncomposted manures should be applied in the fall to outdoor grow sites; they will compost and mellow through the winter while allowing winter rains to leach any salts.

Composted manure can also be used to make a tea to feed your plants during the vegetative stage; there is little chance of burning the plants, so you can be quite generous and feed a manure tea as often as once a week. Hot or fresh manure should be composted before using. Manures are usually available free from small farmers or horse stables.

Mushroom Compost for Tilth

Mushroom compost is not made from mushrooms but for them. Mushroom farms make this compost as a growing medium for commercial mushroom crops. Mushroom compost is normally made in a hot composting process with straw, animal manure, and gypsum. Frequently the materials come from race tracks, where race horses are bedded on oat or wheat straw.

There are usually other nutrients added either while composting or after composting. Many of them are organic in nature, such as blood meal or cottonseed meal, but sometimes there are inorganic additives such as urea.

The one big advantage of mushroom compost is the price; large amounts are incredibly cheap, especially if you pick it up yourself. The fine texture of mushroom compost also makes it easy to dig and work with. Ideally, you will have a mushroom farm close enough to pick it up yourself; generally the farm will load your truck for you. Some farms will give the compost away, but most are now charging a nominal fee for a truckload.

However, mushroom compost does present some problems. Sterilization is one problem with mushroom compost; microbiology is vital for disease prevention, and in supplying nutrients to your plants. Spent mushroom compost lacks these benefits; it is basically dead matter, though it still provides a good substrate and food source for that biology. You can reintroduce microorganisms by mixing with your own compost before applying it, or set it outside and let nature start working on it. Always check with the supplier to make certain they have not used pesticides, and smell the compost before you buy it. If it smells like chemicals, start asking questions.

Another problem is that mushroom compost tends to have a high salt content. This is not necessarily very different from any manure-based compost. Putting the compost outside for a while will allow rain to leach away the salts, or you can speed up the process by watering the pile. Due to the salt content, use mushroom compost to improve tilth in clay soils, but avoid using it too heavily year after year. Eventually you will have too much salt, which will impede the plants' ability to take nutrients from the soil.

There is also the fact that many mushroom composts contain traces of synthetic fertilizers. This will also eliminate it as the preferred compost for yearly application on outdoor grow sites. Do not use mushroom compost as a replacement for good compost, but it is a cheap soil amendment.

Lime for Acidic Soil Control

A good way to stabilize soil pH is to use dolomite lime, or calcium-magnesium carbonate. Dolomite lime acts slowly and continuously, so your soil will remain pH-stable for a few months. It has a pH that is neutral (7.0). When added to soil in the correct proportions, it will stabilize soil at a pH near 7.0.

Use fine size dolomite lime, as the coarser grades take the plant longer to break down and use; they can take a year or longer to work. Fine size dolomite lime is readily available at any garden supply center.

For container growing, add one cup of fine dolomite lime to each cubic foot of soil. Mix the dry soil thoroughly with the dolomite lime, water lightly, and then remix. Recheck the pH after two days.

Wood Ash, Oyster Shells, and Eggshells

Small amounts of hardwood ashes or crushed oyster shells or eggshells will help to raise the soil pH. If you use wood ash, make certain it is from a good hardwood like white oak that you have specifically burned for clean ash. Do not use colored paper or chemical fire starters to start your burn.

Eggshells should be organic and finely ground by processing in a clean coffee grinder. The fine grind will make the shell more quickly available to the plants; it takes much longer to break down big chunks of shell. Oyster shells are available already ground at most garden stores. As with eggshell, a fine grind will make the shell easier for the plants to use more quickly.

Even with gentle amendments like eggshell, wait at least a day or two before checking the pH level of soil after attempting to raise, lower, or stabilize it. If adjustments still have to be made, use small amounts and keep testing. It is easier to add to soil than to try to remove amendments.

Bone Meal

Bone meal is made from animal bones (usually cow bones) that are steamed and then ground. It is an excellent source of phosphorus, which helps with cell division and root growth in plants. Bone meal also contains phosphates, usually about 10 percent.

Bone meal is recommended for its controlled-release form of phosphorus. The nutrients are insoluble in water, so the plants slowly convert it to a form that they can use. Cheaper synthetics offer high levels of phosphorus that are more immediately available to plants, but these are not recommended. Super phosphates are made by treating minerals with acid. They can burn your plants and are not considered organic.

Bone meal is available at almost any garden center. It is quite gentle, so you can be fairly generous when you are mixing your soil. Two or three handfuls can be added to a wheelbarrow load of soil or later scratched into the surface of your plant container.

Blood Meal

Blood meal is exactly what it sounds like: slaughterhouses make dried blood as a byproduct. Blood meal is a high-nitrogen organic plant food (approximately 13 percent), and care should be taken not to apply too much. Soil bacteria break down the blood proteins rapidly to make ammonia. The plant roots absorb the ammonia to take up nitrogen, which is useful during the vegetative phase of cannabis as it adds lots of leafy growth.

Unlike bone meal, blood meal is very acidic, should be used sparingly, and should not be applied to young seedlings. In warm, moist conditions like grow rooms, decomposition can be too rapid, causing ammonia to be released in enough quantity to damage delicate roots.

Blood meal applications last up to four months and should be used with caution: use no more than four ounces per square yard during the growing or vegetative phase. Growers do use it as an element in tea for their plants; dilution with water makes it less likely to burn tender young plants. It can also be used to kick-start a compost pile that has mostly high-carbon ingredients. Some growers also report success in using it to repel deer, attributing the effect to the blood smell. Blood meal is available at all garden stores.

Bat Guano

Bat guano, or bat feces, is a natural superfertilizer and a favorite with cannabis growers. It contains many necessary macro- and micronutrients, as well as a whole host of beneficial microorganisms that cannot be provided by chemical fertilizers. It is considered to be very high in nitrogen, but this can depend on whether the guano comes from insect-eating bats or fruit-eating bats. Fruit eaters produce guano that is higher in phosphorus.

Guano generally consists of ammonia, along with uric, phosphoric, oxalic, and carbonic acids, some earth salts, and a high concentration of nitrates. It supplies nutrients in these approximate amounts: 9 percent nitrogen, 6 percent phosphorus, and 2 percent potassium.

Unless you have a source for guano, like a convenient bat cave, generally the grower must purchase it from an organic garden supplier. It can be quite expensive, but is so beneficial it is worth having.

Many growers stretch their guano dollars by making bat guano tea to feed their plants. Use three tablespoons of bat guano to one gallon of water. Premix the tea in a large bucket using warm (but not hot) water. The warm water breaks down the bat pellets much more efficiently than cold and minimizes stirring. Let the tea steep for at least forty-eight hours before feeding to your plants. Although not strictly necessary, an aquarium pump and air stone will dissolve oxygen into the solution and keep the good bacteria alive and thriving. Let it bubble a day or two before you use it. It is best to feed vegetative plants a cupful directly after watering. If you feed before watering, you may flush out all your good bat guano nutrients. A diluted, nonburning mixture for young plants or seedlings can be made with as little as a tablespoon of guano.

Kelp Meal
Kelp meal (1-0-8) is a dry fertilizer made of iron seaweed and is very high in potassium and trace elements. Kelp meal is an excellent organic source of plant hormones that stimulate plant and root growth. Some cannabis growers use a liquid seaweed (4-2-3) mix for a quick boost for greening foliage and roots. Kelp meal is easily available at garden centers or can be ordered online from organic garden suppliers.

Gypsum
While some growers like to use gypsum to break up heavy clay soils, it is preferable to use compost and other less intense methods to gradually improve your soil. Gypsum is calcium sulphate, and it adds calcium in a somewhat soluble form.

Never use gypsum without testing your soil first. Gypsum should not be applied at all where there is a shallow saline water table and no subsurface drainage; after the excess sodium and magnesium are leached down to the water table, the soil's own capillary action may bring them back to the plants' root zones. If you feel you must use it, gypsum can be found at garden centers. Be sure to read the directions very carefully.

Worm Castings
Worms are natural soil conditioners. They benefit soil structure by loosening soil and improving aeration and drainage. Lots of earthworms are an excellent indication of healthy soil; if your pH is off,

your earthworms will leave. Earthworms should be introduced to compost piles, new beds, and containers whenever possible.

Earthworms derive their nutrition from organic matter in your soil, processing decayed plant parts, decomposing remains of animals, and living organisms like nematodes, protozoans, rotifers, bacteria, and fungi. Earthworms produce their own weight in castings every twenty-four hours. As they digest, many insoluble minerals are converted to a plant-available soluble form, and long-chain molecules such as cellulose are partially broken down by bacteria in the digestive tract. Fresh earthworm casts are several times richer in available nitrogen, available phosphates, and available potash than in the surrounding topsoil. Worm castings also contain many beneficial bacteria and enzymes, making them another favorite of cannabis growers. Most high-end organic potting mixes already contain earthworm castings; check the ingredients when you purchase them, as worm castings are extremely beneficial and useful to your plants.

With any soil amendments, always read labels, especially dilution instructions. Just because something is organic does not mean it will not harm a plant if used in excess.

That being said, most unimproved soils are not ready for prime time; any efforts you make toward creating a near to perfect soil environment will always be rewarded by the ever-obliging cannabis plant. Eventually, as this sort of problem solving becomes familiar to you as a gardener, you will find it exciting to build soil and will evolve your own "perfect" soil mix that is directly suited to your microclimate and your plant strains.

CHAPTER FIVE

PROPAGATION

There are many advantages to breeding your own strains of cannabis and propagating by seed. Cannabis is a very complex plant, and different strains have different benefits for each individual who uses them. You will discover that some strains are what you are looking for, while others are not worth your trouble. Breeding for a certain level of psychoactivity, muscle relaxation, or aroma will allow you to customize your strains for your optimum benefit, in both palatability and effects. Once you have created a strain that pleases you, you can preserve the identical genetics by cloning or asexual propagation.

Propagation of Fixed Hybrids (How to Breed for Seed)

Cannabis produces both male and female plants, with an occasional hermaphrodite thrown in. Ideally the breeder has both parents for observation and can assess for desirable traits to be passed on to the offspring. These include:

- Vigor
- Yield and size
- Hardiness
- Disease resistance

And, specifically:

- Cannabinoid expression
- Taste
- Aroma
- Pain relief

Additionally, ease of manicuring, typical rates of maturation, and color are all of interest to a seed breeder and some of many traits that can be fixed by line breeding.

Here again, the importance of good recordkeeping is imperative; only a few parent individuals will approach the ideal. If your strain wanders from the direction you are trying to take it, you can review the characteristics of the hybrid generations that came before and breed back into the strain for improved performance.

Inbreeding by selecting and crossing individuals that are close to the ideal can produce strains that are fairly close to uniform in six to seven generations. Inbreeding also produces recessive or less than desirable traits in some individuals. These should be removed from the breeding program and not propagated. If inbreeding reduces vigor, the breeder goes back a few generations (another advantage of seed) and back-crosses, or, alternatively, the breeder can introduce another desirable strain into the line.

Accidental pollination will not improve the strain and may even lower or degenerate the strain by random selection of undesirable traits. So whether you are growing inside or outdoors, you must be in control of the pollination process.

Segregation of Male and Female Plants

Your initial little seedlings will be just that, seedlings, with no sexual differentiation at all (unless you've acquired and planted feminized seeds). Your main concern is to provide them with light, water, and plenty of food for strong roots and healthy vegetative growth. At this point, all your seedlings can stay together, although you want to think through how many males you want and where to put them.

They will have to be moved quickly once they provide proof of their sexual determination, or "declare."

The male and female cannabis plants have different flowers that develop from a tiny nub known as the *primordia*, located initially on the main stems. Flowering is triggered by a change in light. This happens naturally outdoors as days grow shorter in the fall. Indoor growers can speed their crop cycles by manipulating the amount of light their plants receive. As a general rule (though genotype may cause some variation), reducing the light period, or photoperiod, to twelve hours—from eighteen or even twenty-four—will trigger flowering.

Site for checking primordia for sexing plants. This is the initial "nub."

The best place to check for flowering is at the top of the plant at the nodes (or intersections) where the plant develops a small leaf spur. The initial primordia will appear behind this spur and will start out looking like a tiny rounded pod.

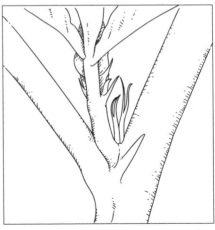

Early female declaration. Note the "hairs" that have come out of the elongated nub.

Eventually the primordia either elongates into a tubular looking female calyx or the more rounded nubbin of the developing male flower. The final proof of sex is the two white hairs or pistils that will appear from the end of the female calyx. These pistils can also appear pinkish or yellowish. It's important to correctly distinguish each plant's sex, so use your jeweler's loupe or magnifying glass to examine the primordia.

Once your plants have declared, you must remove the males at once. Ideally you will have already decided which males to keep for breeding, perhaps even just one.

Early female flower beginning development.

The males can stay in smaller containers, do not need feeding for vegetative growth, and barely need watering. All you want is the pollen, and a tiny (relative to how big the females are going to get) male can produce more than enough for breeding purposes.

Because all you want from the males is their pollen, space is not as much of

Cutting male flowers for pollen collection. Note the extreme difference in the early female and the male flowers.

an issue as it is with the females that you want to grow big and yieldy. Make certain the males will be indoors where they can be severely segregated; absolutely no random pollen transfer should be possible.

When and How to Collect Pollen

The male flowers develop into long hanging clusters of little pods full of pollen and are very pretty to look at. At this point, the male(s) should have been isolated in an area that is easy to seal off, has light, and is not somewhere the household needs to access. Bear in mind, once they start flowering and shedding yellow pollen, you can become a conduit by carrying pollen on your clothing or hands. Keep contact and handling to a minimum, and change your clothing before visiting the girls.

As soon as the male has started the actual release of its bright yellow pollen, cut some branches with good pollen clusters that appear ripe and ready to go. These can stand in tall vases of water set on clean glass or a large mirror. The rest of the plant can be terminated and double bagged for later disposal. If you are using males from different strains, make sure to thoroughly clean your tools and hands in between collecting their pollen to avoid cross-contamination.

Cut male flowers waiting to burst.

Storing Pollen

Scrape the catch off the glass with a clean razor blade and store in very clean, dry glass mason jars, sealed and labeled. Do not touch the pollen with your hands. Make certain only pollen is stored; small parts of the pollen flower or other debris can contain moisture and ruin the delicate pollen with molds. Keep in a cool, dark, dry place until ready to use.

Choosing the Flower to Pollinate

The benefit of selectively breeding by hand is that a female plant can be crossed with one or more male plants to provide seed, and yet most of the female plant will remain seedless. If you are trying more than one cross, make a label for each male so you can identify the breeding later. If you are only working with one male, select a glittery twist tie (the glitter makes them easier to see) for easy marking of the pollinated (or seeder) branch.

Select healthy, well-shaped female flowers on strong axial branches approximately two-thirds of the way down the main trunk of the plant. The flowers can be bred any time after it shows multiple whitish pistils on the cola (female flower). Bear in mind that maturing seed will take between two weeks to five weeks, so plan for an outdoor plant to set seed before your rainy season starts. It is possible to harvest the main plant and leave the seed branch(es) out to finish, but leaving it too late can invite mold.

HASSLE-FREE TIP

Do not choose your top colas for pollination. On a still day, any pollen drift will be downwards. Use the colas on the lower branches to decrease the chance of pollinating more of the plant than you intended.

Pollination Techniques

Pollination is the actual meeting of the pollen with the pistil of the female plant. Germination of the pollen grain requires meeting the ripe pistil and takes approximately ten to twenty minutes after contact. Successful germination results in fertilization (the union of the chromosomes of the parent plants) and is somewhat temperature dependent. In colder weather, fertilization can sometimes take up to two, or even three, days.

In the wild, cannabis is pollinated by wind-borne pollen. This, of course, is not going to work out well for the sinsemilla grower, so extreme care must be taken to prevent accidental release of pollen to the females. Ideally you will pollinate on a still evening; the lack of wind is most important.

Just as with planting seeds, make sure you have time to work slowly and carefully when it comes to pollination. Assemble all your tools ahead of time:

- Labels
- Bags (these should be long, light, narrow paper bags—baguette bags are good)
- Twist ties
- Grafting tape

Review the process before starting. First, pick out and label the branches on the females you will pollinate. There is no need to breed every female you have, but as quirky as nature is, the one plant you do not breed is somehow always one of the best of the crop! So bear that in mind when deciding how many to breed.

Pick strong lower branches with healthy colas. Ideally the female plant should be covered in colas with thick clusters of white pistils and very few brown. Once all the pistils are brown and withered, the reproductive period has passed. Remove most of the large shade leaves from the tips of the chosen branches (this will not hurt the plant).

Second, you will place a very small amount of pollen (⅛ teaspoon is sufficient) in the toe of your bakery bag. Do not shake this around. Pinch the bag shut to contain the pollen until you open it to slip onto the chosen branch. Gently work the bag down the branch and tie with grafting tape to securely seal the bag to the branch. Gently tap the bag and shake the branch to distribute the pollen as evenly as possible.

Leave the bags in place approximately three to four days, then carefully remove them directly into a plastic trash bag and take far away from the grow site to be destroyed. There is still a small chance that viable pollen can escape, so continue to wash your hands and change your clothes after handling. Make certain to sit right down after pollinating and note the date and the crosses in your grow book. Keep an eye on the pollinated branches; you should start to see swelling of the calyxes within the week.

Propagation by Cloning

Remember that when you take a cutting and create a cloned plant, you will be reproducing an exact replica of the genotype. It is important to start with a mother plant or plants of superior quality. There is no improving the strain; what you start with is what you get.

Also bear in mind that having an entire crop of identical clones sets yourself up for more risk of crop failure. The cloned plants are identical, which means they will react to disease and pests in exactly the same way. If the strain you have chosen to reproduce lacks the genetic ability to fight back infections, or is particularly susceptible to molds or mites, you could lose them all. It is strongly advised to have more than one cloned strain in your crop.

Take more cuttings than you are planning to need, as some will possibly fail to develop roots, especially while you are still learning. If you are successful in rooting all your cuttings, you will have a few extra plants to either give away or grow as backups.

How to Take a Cutting

Preparation and organization will make this process easier. Get all your tools ready, and prepare the rooting pots and soil beforehand. Plants will try to heal themselves as rapidly as possible, so leaving cuttings hanging around will greatly lessen your chance of successful rooting. Ideally you will take the cutting with the stem itself in water. If you must wait (for example, if a friend took a cutting and gave it to you), always recut the stem, but this is not ideal. As soon as the stem is cut, an air bubble or embolism can be trapped in the hole in the stem. This will cause the clone to die, as the air bubble blocks fluid flow.

Cloning Essentials

Successful cloning requires the cut stems to have a high carbohydrate level and low nitrogen concentrations. Make certain the mother plant has good drainage and flush the plant with large amounts of water to leach out nitrogen. Do this for three or four days. The nitrogen levels will fall as the plant uses what is available and carbohydrate levels build. Some growers encourage the same process by foliar feeding (feeding through the leaves instead of the roots) with clean water. This is accomplished by heavy misting daily for four days. If the soil of the mother plant has less than ideal drainage, foliar feeding is safer. Heavy soaking of poorly drained soil can cause root rot. As the plant has less nitrogen, growth will slow and the green of older leaves will become lighter.

The clones will also perform better if the cuttings have high levels of root growth hormones. These hormones concentrate mostly at the base of the plant, so take your cuttings from this area close to the main stem or trunk of the mother plant. This is newer growth with the most hormones. It is possible to take cuttings from the top of a plant, but because they have less root growth hormones they'll root very slowly. Generally you can expect cuttings from older growth (the plant tops) to take twice as long to be ready to transplant.

How to Help Your Cutting

Using a rooting hormone also helps the cutting. Although these are available in powder and liquid forms, most cloners seem to prefer using a gel application. Powder forms generally contain talc, which people should avoid breathing.

HASSLE-FREE TIP

Gel rooting hormones such as Clonex are much less messy, require no mixing, and efficiently seal cut tissue. They are much more convenient and quick to use.

If you are organic to the core and want to use a natural hormone booster, try willow water. Willow water has been shown to promote 20 percent more roots than using plain water. Use slim willow branches (approximately one inch in diameter), cut into short lengths and stripped of their leaves. Pack in a clean glass jar, fill with clean water to cover, and soak for twenty-four hours. Pour off the water into smaller jars and let your cuttings soak in willow water for another twenty-four hours, then plant in soil.

Clones perform better at rooting with a pH of 5.0 to 5.5. It is advisable to test the pH if you are planting the cuttings directly into soil or soil and compost mix.

The Cutting Procedure
In addition to the chosen mother plant(s), you will need:

- New, sharp, single-edge razor blades
- Rooting gel
- Alcohol (for sterilizing, not for you)
- Disposable gloves (optional)
- Sharpie pen
- Containers
- Soil or a growing medium like rooting cubes, well moistened

First, decide which females to take cuttings from, and flush the mother plant for three days, if needed. Make certain the mother is at least two months old. Look carefully at the plant and determine how many cuttings you want to take and how many the plant can give you; a lot depends on the actual size of your mother.

HASSLE-FREE TIP
While it is possible to take cuttings from a flowering female plant, it is much easier before the flowering hormones have launched. You will be trying to reverse a powerful force of nature; it can be done, but growers report difficulty and mixed results.

Next, spread out your tools and label the containers for the cuttings. It is best to do the labeling first, especially if you are taking cuttings from more than one mother plant during a session.

Make certain the growing medium is well moistened with a drill premade in the center of the pot or grow cube. You can use a pencil or your little finger, but prepare to accommodate the stem and two trimmed nodes. The drill, or hole, should stop about an inch to a half-inch from the bottom of your container.

Taking cuttings is like a little surgery for your plant; it is very important that everything be quite clean. Wash your hands with soap and hot water, and tools that will touch the cutting should be cleaned with alcohol. Many growers use disposable surgical gloves when they are taking cuttings, but washing your hands well should suffice.

Take the clean razor and make an angled cut on the chosen stem. Remember, you will be taking cuttings from the area close to the main stem or trunk, and near the base. You want a nice clean cut at a forty-five degree angle, not a straight cut. Take three to four sets of leaves in a cut about four inches in length. Immediately place the cut ends in clean water until you are done taking cuttings.

Making an angled cut on the chosen stem.

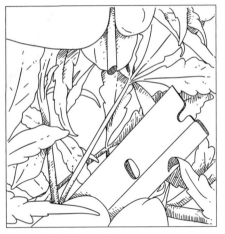

Cutting at a forty-five degree angle.

Next you are going to trim off two sets of leaves and growth nodes nearest to the cut end of the stem while leaving the other two sets of leaves intact. Take your rooting gel and generously apply it to the cut end and all the way up to your trimmed nodes. The rooting gel immediately protects the cuttings and gives them what they need to reroot.

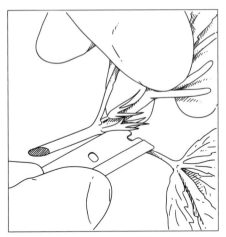

Trimming off two sets of leaves and growth nodes nearest to the cut end of the stem.

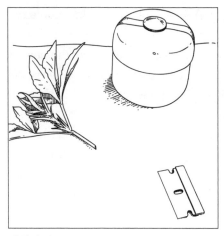

Finished cutting.

Rooting a Cutting

Place the cutting gently into the prepared potting soil or rooting cubes. If you are using soil, fill in with a little soil and water in the cutting. If you are using root cubes, pinch the top of the cube to bring the stem into full contact with the cube.

Keep the cuttings at very high humidity (90 to 100 percent) for the first few days, and then gradually reduce to around 80 percent by the third or fourth day. Some growers use small humidity domes because the cuttings must be kept moist at all times. The domes save a lot of work, as they cut down on the amount of misting you would otherwise need to do. The remaining leaves need to be lightly misted with water for the plant to drink; remember, at this point the cutting has no roots at all and needs to foliar drink until it can grow some.

Clones will root in a small greenhouse, but experienced cloners advise giving eighteen to twenty-four hours of fluorescent light. The little cuttings' leaves are doing all the work for the soon-to-be plant and cannot tolerate intense light. A cool, white light like fluorescent is best.

You can get your clones to root faster if you keep the soil or medium slightly warmer than the air temperature. Some growers use a heating mat, or raise the clone tray up higher and place a light bulb underneath for warmth.

The clones should perk up within a few days to a week. If they stay wilted after seven days, they are probably not going to make it. Sometimes you will have to cull these nonachievers, as leaving them wilting amongst the healthy clones can lead to disease. The cuttings that have rooted successfully should be ready to transplant in one to three weeks. Check to see if there is healthy looking root growth from the grow cube or bottom of the little pot.

Once you have healthy white roots growing at least an inch and a half long from the cube, you can transplant your rooted clone and proceed with vegetative growth. Remember not to shock it by sudden exposure to bright and hot light (whether from the sun or grow lights); gradually lower the fluorescent lights to within a few inches of the clones to get them ready for more and hotter light.

CHAPTER SIX

CANNABIS IN CONTAINERS

An outdoor container garden can be grown on a deck or interspersed with other cover/companion plantings within your regular garden. This can be one of the best ways to start off growing cannabis. It allows you to try growing without a large outlay in labor and materials, and allows easy moving of the plants as you learn how the sun moves around your property during the growing season.

Considerations

If you are thinking of a small outdoor grow in containers, the first things to look at are how close your neighbors are and how accessible your deck or backyard garden is to passersby. Ideally this area is fenced, with a locking gate.

Light

Another big factor in urban or suburban grows is the presence of artificial light. Do your neighbors have nighttime security lights or bright porch lights? Are there streetlights on all night? Cannabis's flowering is triggered by light cycle, whether natural seasonal duration of the sunlight or by artificial light, so continuous nighttime light can be a problem.

Proximity to Schools

Check into the laws in your particular state; many legal medical growers have been dismayed to find out that growing (even indoors) within 1,000 feet of a school is a prohibited activity. This is something far better known ahead of time, as the legal implications can be very troublesome.

Potential Thieves

Even if you are growing legally on your own property, remember that your cannabis will be very attractive to thieves. The best way to protect your plants is to have them blend in to an existing container garden or a mix of containers and larger varied plants that are perennial, larger, and growing in the ground.

An array of different greens and leaf types (think of how camouflage works) makes it much harder for the nongardener to spot cannabis. Most cannabis thieves are not gardeners; that is why they are out stealing yours!

Container Types

There is an enormous variety of useful containers available. Pick your containers based on availability, cost, and efficiency. The size of containers you use for mature cannabis plants will, in part, be determined by how big you can allow the plants to get. If you live in a suburban townhouse and are growing a few on your deck, you will want to keep the plants small to avoid detection and theft. Cannabis plants are somewhat like goldfish; they will generally grow to fit their space. A ten-foot sativa towering on your balcony will be noticed by even the most unobservant passerby.

Small Containers

Say you plan to grow four plants on your deck. You have access to water, and ideally already have some general plants out there, including herbs and container tomatoes. To simplify, you start with clones, so you know they are females. You have identified the sunniest spot and checked that taller buildings do not overlook your deck.

> ↓ **LOW-CO$T TIP**
> The least expensive way to go is to use recycled nursery pots. These can come from a friend who has recently purchased and ground-planted large shrubs, or nurseries will frequently give used plastic pots away or sell them for a nominal fee. Ones used for baby trees can be quite large; up to fifteen or twenty gallons in size.

If you are using recycled pots, give them a thorough cleaning, including wiping with a light bleach solution and then rinsing with clear water. This will eliminate any harmful fungi or bacteria that may have been in the previous soil. Most nursery pots lack enough drain holes, so take a drill to the bottom and double the drain holes. Put in a bottom layer of drain rock to improve drainage.

Since you are keeping your plants small, go for the five-gallon pots; the taller variety seems to work better than the shorter, fatter version. They both hold five gallons of soil, but the taller pots suit the growing style of the cannabis a bit better. Of course, if all you can find are the shorter pots, cannabis will accommodate you and adjust itself accordingly.

Wine Barrels

Another, more elegant, solution for containers is recycled oak wine barrels. In the early heyday of cannabis growing in 1970s Mendocino County, wine barrels were cheap. Now wine barrels are sold as half barrels for $20 and up.

While wine barrels are attractive, breathe well, and have excellent drainage, they are also expensive, hard to clean, and will eventually rot. If you are going to use half barrels, make certain to get your drill out and make multiple drain holes in the bottom. The wine barrels hold more soil, so be prepared for your plants to get quite large.

HASSLE-FREE TIP

It might seem obvious, but be careful and think ahead when using power tools to make drain holes. Drilling through the bottom of a container is simple until you figure out you just drilled through too far and made holes into your (or your landlord's) nice deck. Flip the container over for this activity!

Plastic Barrels

Less elegant, but much cheaper and lighter to move when empty, are food-grade thirty-gallon plastic shipping barrels. Each barrel can be cut in half to yield two containers. The plastic is very tough and yet easy to drill through and cut. They must be rated food grade, which means they originally contained something like soy sauce, not motor oil. Typically, the whole barrel will cost somewhere between $8 and $15. The plastic barrels will last for years, unlike the similar-sized oak half barrel.

It is advisable to paint the outside surface with natural colors (various greens or light browns—think camouflage again) so the barrels don't stand out too much. If you are planting a mixed garden totally in barrels, this is less of an issue. You do not want to have just the cannabis in bright containers, as it will draw attention specifically to the cannabis. You want the cannabis plants to blend in with your other garden plants.

Again, as with the wine half barrels, the plants will get quite large with so much growing space. Outdoor growers who have vole or gopher problems with direct-ground planting frequently use food-grade barrels. The barrels can be half-buried in the ground for less visibility. If you do this, be sure to make extra drain holes, as the barrel will drain more slowly when buried. If voles or gophers are a problem, place a protective screen of chicken wire over the surface of the half-buried barrel; this will prevent pocket gophers or voles burrowing into your container from the top.

Grow Bags

Grow bags are another economically sound container solution for the grower. The main disadvantage is the need to support the bag and plant as the plants get large. These are mainly advised for the grower with a larger crop. They also come prepacked with peat or compost, so you have less control over your soil mix. Peat-free composts are improving, but most people still find peat bags give the best results.

If you are starting out in coldish spring weather, warm the bags. Either store inside a heated room for a few days or cover with black plastic sheeting in the sun. This will take the chill off and warm the compost. Young plants crave warmth. Preferably wearing gloves, shake the bags hard to loosen the compost and prick the bottoms with a knife or a garden fork for drainage before putting them in their planting positions.

One disadvantage of grow bags, unlike hard pots or barrels, is their need for support. You can either set up supports for tall plants against a wall, hammer stakes into the ground around the grow bag, or purchase a self-supporting grow bag frame. You will also need to position your watering aids before planting. Trying to do this later will disturb the plant's roots and slow growth.

Once the bags are set up, cut a cross in the center of the top of the bag the size of the plant's interim pot, peel back the plastic, unpot the plant, and plant. Cut pot-sized crosses in the top of the bag between your centered plant spot and sink a 4-inch plastic plant pot into the compost up to its rim in each position. Direct the water and feed into these pots and it will quickly soak down to the bottom of the bag.

HASSLE-FREE TIP

If you have more than a few bags, it is worth investing in a drip feed watering system with a timer. Cannabis has an enormous appetite for water and will quickly fill the bag with roots, which, unlike soil, do not retain water. Bags can dry out much more rapidly than barrels.

Smart Pots Aeration Containers

Smart Pots aeration containers are a recent innovation in containers that are being used very successfully by many growers. They are made from a super strong black fabric material that warms up quickly in the spring, giving the plants a friendly environment for rapid growth. The porous nature of the fabric provides excellent breathability, favorable for root development, and allows heat to escape through evaporative cooling when the weather gets hot. The fabric also drains very well.

Of interest to the outdoor grower is that the fabric base will contour to and establish capillary contact with the soil. Of interest to both outdoor and indoor growers, Smart Pots come in many sizes from small to very large, so you can customize to fit your growing space.

Raised Beds

Depending on space and privacy considerations, the grower might consider a large raised bed. The advantages are many: lots of food and good drainage, yet the roots are protected from burrowing rodents by the wire bottom of the container. The extra height makes for greater ease in working on the plants, and the grower maintains control over the soil mix.

Four large cannabis plants can be grown in an eight foot by eight foot raised bed. If you have sufficient sunlight and pay attention to feeding and watering, normally expect a yield of a pound to a pound and a half from each plant. You will need:

- A roll of chicken wire or similar mesh size metal (heavier gauge is fine).
- 12 heavy (8 × 8 preferably) eight-foot posts. Railroad tie is not recommended, as it has been soaked with creosote to prevent

wood rotting. If you must use railroad tie, enclose the inside of the bed with flashing or heavy-duty black plastic so the plants do not come in contact with it.

- ¾" drain rock (enough to cover square footage two or three inches in depth).

Prep Work

First, plan for the seasonal movement of the sun, and mark out your square. Second, check the soil drainage where you plan to locate the bed. Do a small perc test by digging a few small holes to one foot in depth and fill with water. Monitor to see how quickly water drains. If it stands for hours like it is in a bucket, you have poor drainage and probably compacted clay soil. If you have a small garden tiller, do a light pass over the square to improve drainage; otherwise, do a little aerating with your garden fork.

Assembling Your Raised Bed

Of course, if the soil is already well drained, proceed to spread the drain rock evenly within the square, and lay your wire bottom out flat. If you are using chicken wire, it will tend to curl back into its roll form as you struggle to spread it out. Have the wire overlap the outside dimension of the enclosure by two to three inches. Have some heavy rocks or soil sacks to weight the ends until you start stacking your walls. The walls will then hold the wire in place.

Using a heavier gauge rigid panel type of wire is easier to work with alone, as you can just lay the flat panels down. Make sure the holes are no larger than the ones in chicken wire to keep out voles.

Stack the sides of the raised container. Figure a minimum of sixteen inches in height. If you want to go higher and have the soil resources to fill the container, go right ahead. If you prepare the raised bed in the fall, you can stack it with manure and mulch the top with spoiled hay to mellow through the winter. In the spring you can till in all the site-made compost; all winter the nutrients have been bathed with rainfall and composting in your bed. A garden fork is all you will need to work the bed, although some growers have tiny tillers.

The containers you decide to use will depend on your budget and your ingenuity; growers are continually finding new sources for earth-containing cannabis homes. There is no right way or wrong way, as long as you remember drainage is a key factor with containers.

Container Soil

A container-grown plant is far more dependent on you for food than a plant that grows in in the ground. Even if they are fed on schedule, the ground-planted cannabis can seek out nutrients. The container plant has a much smaller and rigidly limited environment; they react much more quickly if you forget or delay a feeding.

Once your little seedlings are up, they are working hard at building healthy roots and making large green leaves for efficient photosynthesizing. Photosynthesis is the process your plants use to combine sunlight, water, and carbon dioxide to produce oxygen and sugar (energy). Your soil mix must provide enough food for the plants to work with.

The right soil mix is essential to produce large, green, and happy plants. Cannabis is a fast grower and big feeder. It is much more sensible to plan ahead and not wait until the plant is frantically signaling you that it needs food or that its drainage is poor.

If you are working with clones, put the plants in their final containers right away. If you are starting from seed and must deal with the sexual differentiation phase, you will not have the space, time, money, or inclination to put each little seedling into a big grow container. Until they declare male or female, you will be monitoring them in three- to five-gallon containers and feeding them frequently. If you are growing indoors, a three- to five-gallon container may be the largest your plants will get. Indoor growers have limited space and do not necessarily want the garden to outgrow its room.

Consider the Soil

The basic requirement for all cannabis is nutrient-rich, well-drained soil. If you are not a gardener already, you may want to start out using really good, bagged potting soil. Some gardeners mix their own because they have control over ingredients and amendments. And, of course, there is the question of cost. There are various kinds available at garden centers, but do not be swayed by price alone. A cheap mix will be heavy on the perlite (not that perlite is bad, in fact, it is very good for drainage, but it contains no nutrients at all).

It is also important to note that many potting mixes are made to support an average-size houseplant in a small pot. They are frequently manufactured entirely from wood and bark fiber, composts, and soil conditioners, with a light, fluffy texture. This texture requires the addition of sandy loam to make cannabis happy. Additionally, these mixes seldom contain enough nutrients to support healthy cannabis growth for more than a few months, if even that long.

Starter Mixes

A good starter mix is one-third sandy loam for drainage, one-third compost you have made, and one-third organic bagged soil. If your grow is small, or cost is no object, a mix of the FoxFarm Ocean Forest Potting Soil is really the way to go. If you plan to mix soil, sandy loam can be purchased in bulk at some garden centers and by the yard at rural feed and fuels.

You should screen all your soil through a compost screen; this will remove lumps and bits of wood or other compost components that have not broken down.

The discard materials can be thrown back on your compost pile or used for mulch around other garden plants. Once you have screened your components, the soil will be easy to mix. It is easiest to screen and mix by the wheelbarrow load; the wheelbarrow makes a convenient mixing bowl and you can make certain all components are blended before filling your containers. Wear gloves and a mask while you screen and mix, especially if the materials are dry enough to be dusty.

Water in the Soil

Once you have filled your containers with the carefully blended, screened soil mix, you need to gently water the soil and mix lightly to eliminate dry spots. Fill the container to standing water three times; note the water coming from the drain holes. This should ensure that the soil mix is evenly dampened.

Plant Your Seedlings

Prepare a hole slightly deeper than the pot the seedling currently sits in, scratch in a small handful of bone meal, unpot, and gently place the seedling in the hole. It is better to transplant when the seedling's soil is slightly dry; soil that is wet can break apart and take some of the seedling's root system with it. Fill in around the seedling and gently but firmly press it into the soil; this will make for good soil contact for the roots and helps the plant transition more easily. Water the seedling and gently press it in place one more time. Ideally, transplanting should be done in early morning or in the evening so seedlings are not shocked by the hot noontime sun.

Fertilizing

If you start out with pure high-end bagged soil or create a similar blend on your own, there is really no need to initially feed too much extra if the containers are large. A small handful of bone meal worked into the planting hole will start each young plant off with good root-building food, and the plant will draw what it needs from the soil.

A manure tea can be fed once a week after watering; manure teas are so gentle that some growers feed each time they water. If your plants have a healthy green foliage and are growing vigorously, they are getting what they need. Stay alert for narrowing of leaves or yellowing in color; the plants are signaling they need food. Bear in mind that indicas tend to have very dark green leaves, and sativas are a paler green, like healthy bamboo. Do not mistake a genetic trait for a plant problem. Plants that are hungry for nitrogen will pale; feed with manure tea and observe them. If you were correct, the plants should respond within three to four days.

Figure on using about a gallon of composted manure to four gallons of water to brew manure teas. Some kinds of manure are higher in nitrogen than others (bat guano is one of the highest), so you can adjust your blend slightly as you see how your plants respond.

If you use packaged fertilizers or ones you need to mix before applying, remember to use only organics, and know that more is not better. Read and follow instructions carefully to prevent burning your plants.

Watering

Remember, rooftops or decks can be much windier than gardens closer to the ground; wind dries out plants and soil, so these sites will require more and closer moisture monitoring. Also, plan ahead and bear in mind that large containers of soil can get extremely heavy when fully watered, either by you or by rain. Make certain your deck or rooftop can safely take the weight of your container garden.

HASSLE-FREE TIP
A moisture meter is an invaluable aid in checking how much water your plants need. These are readily available at your local garden supply, starting at under $5.

The amount and how you water in container gardening will have a large effect on how well your cannabis plants grow. Cannabis likes to dry out a little bit between waterings—the soil should just be starting to pull away from the rim of the containers. Then you need to water slowly with a gentle stream from your hose. The goal is to have the water gradually permeate the soil mix all over, not to create channels of least resistance where water runs down and out.

Watering ten large cannabis plants in twenty-gallon containers can take a lot longer than you might think. An egg timer is a useful tool for watering; you can start the water going and come back to check at fifteen-minute intervals. The container should fill and drain down three times to ensure that the plant is watered thoroughly. Just damping the top surface of the soil may look good, but the lower part of the container soil will be dry as a bone, and leave your plants unhappy and thirsty.

Depending on weather conditions (extra hot, or windy, or rainy and cool), you will have to vary your watering schedule. Stick a finger into the soil near the plants' roots. Is the soil damp from dew and extremely dry underneath? You need to know before the plants show stress.

During the phase of vegetative growth, it is fine for the outdoor grower to spray the plants leaves off after watering in the evening. This will knock off most unwanted insects and refresh the plants after a long hot day. Do not overhead water cannabis as a general practice: the plants do not like or require it, and you risk burning the leaves if the sun is high and hot.

Container gardening of cannabis is a fun and relatively easy way to start out as a grower, and most indoor growers have to use containers. It is a good way to protect plants from bad soils and burrowing animals, and it is extremely productive if done correctly.

CHAPTER SEVEN

CANNABIS INDOORS

Although some people in urban areas still grow a few cannabis plants in their vegetable gardens, generally the urban cannabis farmer is forced to grow inside. In the medical-use states, this is not because of law enforcement but because of thieves. Prohibition continues to make cannabis extremely expensive for those who must purchase it on the black market.

The Advantages

Indoor growing does have some advantages, especially if the grower lives in a geographic area that has very short growing seasons. Indoor growers are less tied to their crops; during the season, an outdoor grower must always be on site or risk losing his cannabis. Indoor growers can check the grow room in the morning and drive off to work. As long as they have been discreet about their growing activities, there is usually very little to alert thieves that valuable cannabis is inside.

Indoor growers have far less worry about accidental pollination of their prize female plants; unless they place a male in the grow room or carry pollen into the plants on their clothes, they are guaranteed pure sinsemilla, or seedless, female plants. Outdoor growers, of course, must worry about wind-borne pollen that may have traveled silently and invisibly to the grow site. Although useable, seeded cannabis is not considered of high value and is usually harsher to smoke.

The indoor grower's crop is almost never bothered by wildlife bigger than a spider mite. Deer, roving livestock, burrowing rodents, or wood rats cannot access your prized plants.

Another aspect of indoor growing is the ability to always have a crop in cycle. Once the outdoor season is over, the outdoor grower has the entire year's harvest. An indoor grower can produce a crop every ten to twelve weeks. Crop failures or theft are still annoying and expensive, but the indoor grower has the option to start again immediately.

Problems to Consider

One of the biggest problems of growing cannabis indoors is the expense. The grow room or rooms must be constructed properly. Most indoor growers have a vegetative room and a flowering room so that they can keep a crop in cycle at all times. The equipment for lights, ventilation, humidity, and odor-control requires a large initial outlay. The power bills to keep the artificial environment running are prohibitive. Having a productive indoor grow is a costly investment.

Another thing to consider is space. You will lose personal space in your home after you designate an area for grow rooms, or face the expense of building and maintaining a special building for your growing activities. If you have a large basement in your house, or unused outbuildings, this is less of a problem.

The other huge problem for indoor growers is keeping the grow rooms clean and pest free; spider mites are the number one enemy of the indoor cannabis grow. The artificial environment tends to preclude assistance from nature, a very large and powerful helper indeed.

Another downside to having your grow actually within your home is that your home is where you live. If home invasion thieves come in for your cannabis, you are in there with it. Cannabis thieves can be armed and willing to kill for the financial value of your crop. The outdoor grower may lose his crop, but he can choose whether to confront thieves. In medical cannabis states, law enforcement is mandated to respond and protect the grower; an outdoor grower can monitor a situation from inside his home and call the police for help.

What if you are not a licensed medical grower? If law enforcement gets a warrant to come in your home, you, your family, and your pets may be in great danger not only because of possible arrest and incarceration, but also of being in the line of fire. This danger, plus the odds that your home will be trashed, greatly increases when the police perform a raid on an indoor grow.

The final disadvantage of an indoor grow is that it is far less productive than an outdoor grow for a great deal more use of diminishing world resources. Even if the financial expense is not an issue, the indoor cannabis grower must reflect and consider the immense use of fossil fuels to produce a relatively small amount of cannabis.

Materials

The basic and essential materials you will need to grow cannabis indoors are as follows:

- A prepared space to grow in, or grow room
- Lights
- Fans
- Odor-control system, usually carbon filtered
- Air intake and exhaust system
- Thermometer
- Hygrometer
- Pots or containers
- Soil or soilless growing medium
- Soil amendments
- Cannabis cuttings, seeds, clones, or seedlings

The Grow Room

Most indoor growers start out with a single grow room; this makes sense until you decide if indoor growing is for you. The high-production approach uses two grow rooms. One is for the vegetative stage of the cannabis life cycle, and the other is a flowering room. Using two rooms lets the indoor grower continually cycle and harvest cannabis. Using one room mimics the outdoor cycle on an immensely speeded-up time frame.

Make certain the grow area has access to electrical outlets in good working condition. You will be placing a lot of power load on the electrical system, and many an indoor grow has gone up in flames when the electrical setup was done casually or too cheaply. Remember, this is usually also where you live, so you could lose far more than just your cannabis.

Venting

The space should be vented, as big lights generate a lot of heat. Separate exhaust and incoming air vents are best—one at the top of the room to exhaust air into the attic or out the roof, and one to bring in air from an outside wall or crawlspace.

Odor Control

Cannabis plants emit a strong and distinctive odor during their reproductive phase. This can alert thieves or law enforcement that you are growing cannabis, as eventually this odor is vented to the outside of your house. It can also permeate the inside of a home, again leading casual visitors to either wonder what the smell is or to know what the smell is, which can be worse depending on their views about cannabis.

Most indoor growers eliminate the odor danger by forcing the grow room air through a carbon filter. Many home cultivators simply attach a large carbon filter to their air extraction system and filter any smell before the air is expelled from the grow room.

Another way of eliminating odor is by installing an ozone generator in the extraction ducting. Air is forced past the ozone generator by the extraction fan, and the air is neutralized as it mixes with the ozone.

If you are going to need any ducting or electrical work done by an outside repairman, plan ahead and get this done first, before your growing area looks like anything but a basement, potential shop, or art room. You do not have to discuss anything with a contractor, but casual conversation about a pottery studio can deflect any speculation you are setting up a cannabis grow.

Room Prep

Once you select the location and have the electrical and exhaust systems figured out, you need to prepare it. First, completely clean the room. Floors need to be thoroughly cleaned, and the walls should also be sprayed with a light bleach solution and wiped down.

Any windows in the grow area must be covered completely and checked from outside at night for light loss. Unless they are made of concrete, the floors should be covered in plastic to prevent water damage. You will be gardening in this room, and water spills can happen. Whether the floor is yours or your landlord's, you do not want to create a mold-inducing environment from wet wood or soaked tile grout.

Paint the walls flat white, choosing paint with high titanium dioxide content to maximize reflectivity. Some indoor growers cover the walls of their grow room with some type of reflective material. The most common is 6 mil (150 μm) PVC plastic sheeting that is white on the room side and black to the wall. The white side reflects light, and the black side reduces mold growth. Other common coverings are Mylar sheeting and Astrofoil, both of which reflect heat. There is also the option of Foylon, a foil-laminated, reinforced fabric that some growers use successfully. Some indoor growers have also experimented with using tin foil to intensify light. This is not advised, as the foil can actually focus light into hot beams and burn holes through the plants' leaves.

A broad, well-secured shelf above the main grow area can be used to root cuttings and germinate seedlings. The area will stay very warm, eliminating the need for a germination warming pad. If you are only using one grow room, hang a lightproof curtain to separate the shelf from the main area when the lights are on flowering cycle settings.

Lights

Lumen is a measurement of light output. It refers to the amount of light emitted by one candle that falls on one square foot of surface located at a distance of one foot from the candle. Traditionally, lumens have been the benchmark of a lamp's ability to grow plants, meaning the brighter the lamp, the better the plant performs. However, studies have shown that using a broader color spectrum lamp causes much better plant growth than a lamp with high-lumen output.

High-intensity discharge (HID) is a special type of lighting that is intensely bright. An HID lighting system consists of a ballast, reflector, socket, and lamp (light bulb). The ballast acts like the engine, converting and driving energy to illuminate the lamp. HID lighting options for plant growth are typically metal halide (MH) or high-pressure sodium (HPS) systems.

Metal halide lamps provide more of the blue/green spectrum, which is ideal for plants that are in a vegetative stage. MH lamps provide a more natural appearance in color and are typically for plants that have no natural light available. Cannabis can do very well grown full cycle under MH, but get daylight halide for best results.

HPS lamps provide more yellow/orange/red spectrum, which is perfect for plants that are actively flowering. Ideally, the indoor grower would use MH to grow his plants and HPS to flower his plants, but either choice is quite suitable for the entire cycle.

Traditionally, fluorescent lighting was used for seedlings, cuttings, and plants with low light-level requirements, and HID was used for established plants and plants with higher light-level requirements. Advances in fluorescent lighting technology have provided more options for indoor growers. T5 fluorescent lighting is the latest in plant-growth lighting. T5's high light output combined with low heat and energy consumption makes it another light source choice for the indoor cannabis grower.

Your budget will decide how complex your initial lighting and ventilation setups can be. If you are growing medically, many compassion centers have used lighting setups available for reasonable prices. Always do your research, and visit indoor agricultural stores and ask questions. Indoor growing technology is changing radically and rapidly.

↓ LOW-CO$T TIP

An easy way to figure out your projected power bill for grow room lights is to multiply the grow room's total bulb wattage times the number of hours of operation and divide by 1,000. This figure is the number of kilowatt-hours of electricity used. (Example: a 400-watt lamp running for 18 hours will use 7.2 kilowatt-hours.) Check your power bill for the cost of each kilowatt-hour. Then multiply the number of kilowatt-hours used by the cost of a kilowatt-hour (K/hr) to figure the cost to run your light for that many hours.

Containers

Most indoor cannabis growers use containers that hold between two and five gallons of soil—a good compromise in terms of weight, space, and cost. They can be moved easily and hold an adequate reservoir of water and nutrients to support a large indoor plant.

You can calculate the right size containers to use by the amount of light per square foot. For a moderate light, or 15 to 25 watts per square foot, you should use a minimum of one-gallon containers but preferably three-gallon containers. For plants receiving more light, or over 25 watts per square foot, use at least three-gallon containers but preferably eight-gallon containers. The containers must have several holes in the bottom to assure drainage. Growers typically use black plastic nursery pots, but you can use flowerpots, plastic buckets, small trash cans, or plastic grow bags.

The Soil

In its natural state outdoors, cannabis can grow an extensive root system, especially in dry areas where the main taproot can grow more than six feet deep in its search for water. Cannabis also has a fibrous network of fine, lateral roots that branch off the main taproot. In moister environments with nutrient-rich soil, the lateral roots are able to supply water and nutritive needs, and the taproot can remain small; cannabis will adjust to the indoor grow's space limitations as long as you feed and water properly.

Natural Soil

The growing medium is important. It serves as a source for water, air, and nutrients, and must also anchor the plant's roots. Cannabis has high water and nutritive needs and grows very fast, unlike most houseplants. The indoor grow room is also an unnatural environment. Natural controls for harmful soil bacteria and insects must be replaced by the gardener's attention and care.

The texture of the medium determines how well it holds water and how well it drains. Cannabis requires a well-drained medium for healthy growth. Soils that hold too much water can drown the roots leading to poor growth, or may even kill the plants. Well-drained soil allows roots access to air as well as water. Soils that are dense clay, or too rich in compost that holds too much water, will not have enough air. Soilless media, like perlite, drains almost too well but contains no nutrients.

The soil must be nutrient-rich to satisfy the heavy feeding needs of cannabis. Some gardeners are adamant about using their own soil mixes because they have control over ingredients and amendments, but if you are just starting out, take advantage of a good quality pre-mix. There are various kinds of bagged soils available at garden centers, but beware of cheap mixes. A cheap mix will be fluffy in texture and heavy on the perlite. Not that perlite is bad; in fact, it is very good for drainage, but it contains no nutrients at all. These mixes seldom contain enough nutrients to support healthy cannabis growth for long. Their nitrogen (N) is usually too low, phosphorus (P) level is adequate, and the potassium (K) level is usually very high.

It is far better to pay the higher price and use an organic bagged soil like FoxFarm Ocean Forest Potting Soil. A mix of the Ocean Forest quality has the correct texture for good drainage and is already preloaded with ideal nutrients for the vegetative phase cannabis plant. Black Gold makes an organic potting soil that is adequate, but for cannabis it needs adjustment with sandy loam; the texture is too fluffy; and, additionally, it contains less specialized organic nutrients than the more expensive mixes.

Soilless Soil

Some indoor growers prefer to use a soilless medium and feed nutrients to their plants, or use a mix that includes real soil. These media can improve a natural soil that has poor drainage characteristics.

Perlite is expanded sand or volcanic glass. It is almost weightless, contains no nutrients, and is near neutral in pH. Perlite mixed with real soil can hold water, air, and nutrients from the soil, and it is particularly good at aerating heavy soil.

Vermiculture is also near neutral in pH. It, too, holds water, air, and nutrients well and will improve the texture of sandy or fast-draining soils. Jiffy Mix, Ortho Mix, or similar mixes are made of ground vermiculite and sphagnum moss and are fortified with a small amount of nutrients.

Peat moss (also sometimes called sphagnum moss) is sometimes used by growers to improve water holding and texture. Used in excess, it tends to make the medium too acidic after a few months of watering. As a soil amendment, peat moss breaks down too fast, compressing the soil, and creating an unhealthy lack of air for plant roots. Environmentally conscious growers use alternative products.

Choosing the Best Strains

Modern indoor cannabis breeders have spent years modifying plant characteristics to optimize quality and adapt to the indoor methods of production. Cannabis competitions have created international arenas for breeders to compare accomplishments and to market their strains to the world.

Some strains remain classics and are available for years. Others are improved upon and become harder to find as growers continue to refine flavor, aroma, and effects. Cannabis strain development and the ability to procure different recreational strains rise and fall with the fads and fashions, sometimes driven by clever marketing and publicity.

The best seed sites will list their strains like a good garden catalog. They list provenance, typical characteristics of the strain in appearance, preferred growing conditions, and the qualities of the end product, usually both for productivity and effects. This is very useful if you have limited space and need reliable information about results you can expect from your grow.

Some well-known strains that are known to grow easily and well for indoor growers include:

- Silver Haze is a tall plant for indoors, due to a mainly sativa background. Silver Haze is a cross of a sativa, Purple Haze, to a nondominant indica. The indoor breeder's goal was to minimize height and flowering time of the typical sativa but still retain the unique sativa psychoactive effect.
- Kush is a pure indica and is a short, compact plant. A two-time winner of the international Cannabis Cup, Kush is very popular among indica growers.
- New York Diesel is an Afghani/sativa hybrid. This strain is considered good for beginning growers because it is very disease resistant and tends to grow uniformly.
- Northern Lights is another short, compact plant with big broad leaves and large flowers. This strain is considered a classic and is easy to grow.
- Big Bud is also a classic and was the Cannabis Cup winner in 1989 as a best strain. The yield is legendary, producing massive flowers.

Name That Strain

The U.S. Patent Office seemed to pave the way to allow growers to trademark their own marijuana strains when it opened a federal trademark category entitled "Processed plant matter for medicinal purposes, namely medical marijuana." However, the patent office recently closed that door because marijuana is still federally illegal. So while you may not be able to claim a legal trademark for your own Portland Pete strain, it also means that no one can trademark and own the rights to popular strains such as Purple Haze and Northern Lights.

The Growing Cycle (Brief)

The beginning of the cycle is procuring clones or starting your seeds. These little ones will need to be nurtured until they are of big enough size to be transplanted to big containers. The word "clone" can actually be a little vague. A clone does not have to be the size of a cutting; this is just when growers generally receive them from the propagator. Sometimes a clone arrives as a three- or four-foot-tall plant, a happy bonus. You may also have to root some cuttings to get started. Plan on two to four weeks for the cuttings to root and become actual little plant clones. Once you have little plants, you want your grow room lights to cycle for the vegetative phase. Make sure the plants get eighteen hour "days" and six hour "nights" for two full weeks.

The first transplant for seedlings is usually from their little four-inch starter pots to a three- or five-gallon container. This will allow enough room for the plants to grow while they make their sexual determination. Clones are known females, so the grower can put them right into his largest container.

The plants will be in what is called the vegetative phase of growth. This is when plants grow roots, gain size, and build strong stems and lots of healthy green leaves. Cannabis is light sensitive and requires a light trigger to begin the phase of flower development so desired by cannabis growers. During the vegetative phase, the plants will need plenty of water and more nitrogen than during the flowering phase.

If the grower plans to make clones from this crop, now is the time to take cuttings. It is possible to clone from a flowering plant, but this is not advised. It takes the cutting far longer to root, and the new little plant may try to flower right away.

The plants will grow until the seventh week, when the indoor grower should shorten the light cycle from eighteen-hour days and six-hour nights to twelve hours of each. This is the sign or trigger to the plants that the days remaining for reproduction are becoming fewer. The plants will begin flowering in an attempt to reproduce, which is their natural goal. Some growers report that giving the plants an initial thirty-six hours of darkness before starting the twelve/twelve light cycle will shorten the time it takes for flowering to appear.

If the grower plans to breed for seed, she will have isolated a male or males of preferred lineage and collected and labeled their pollens. As soon as the female plants show pistils, the grower can pollinate selected branches to create new hybrids and fresh seed.

As the plants grow flowers, their vegetative growth will slow and then stop. They are concentrated on reproduction, and a large array of healthy, resin-covered flowers is their chance to catch pollen. The plants do not know they are in a grow room and will produce resins as fast as they can. At this time the grower stops feeding nitrogen and increases the ratio of phosphorus and potassium that the plants need for flowering.

During this phase, the careful grower spends quite a bit of time grooming the plants by removing yellowed leaves, clearing any plant debris that falls to the floor, and keeping a sharp eye out for mold on the flowers. Different hybrids will complete their flowering at different times, but generally the end of the twelfth week in the cycle will be harvest time. As with outdoor cannabis, the indoor grower monitors trichomes (fine, hairlike growth from the buds) to estimate the amount of finish on the harvest.

Harvesting Indoor Plants

Since indoor plants are much smaller than outdoor grown plants, one person can easily harvest them. Some indoor growers harvest in sections to give less finished parts of the plants a chance to produce more resins, or for their own convenience. As always, monitor the color of the trichomes to check for the optimum harvest moment.

As soon as your harvest comes into the drying area, start using your oscillating fans at once. The fans should be placed to maximize airflow around the hanging plants while avoiding a direct blast continually blowing on them. Avoid having the fans positioned too low as they may blow up dust from the shed floor. As the green (or "wet") plants are cut up and hung to dry, the earliest settings can be on high. As the plants dry out more, lower the fan settings to maintain a gentle continual cycling of air. The dried flowers can be used within a few weeks, but really should be hung to cure for four to eight weeks (depending on moisture in the air, thickness of colas, and the temperature of your drying room). After the hanging plants are manicured, curing will continue for up to three or four months. It is important to monitor the bags or jars where the cannabis is stored. At least once a week, breathe the containers and test the taste. Do not seal uncured cannabis or you will ruin the taste and have a very harsh finish to your product.

CHAPTER EIGHT

THE GROWING CYCLE (INDOORS)

There are a large number of cannabis growers who grow their plants indoors. Many, if not most, grow indoors because they cannot risk exposing their plants to potential thieves. Some indoor growers prefer to control the plants' environment. Licensed cannabis growers in medical states are also frequently forced indoors. They, too, cannot risk losing their crop to thieves, especially because the cannabis is medicine that patients rely on receiving regularly. There are many indoor growers who are not really gardeners but producers of a product by artificial methods.

Light and Space Requirements

Currently, the most commonly used lighting for indoor grow rooms is high-intensity discharge (HID) lighting. As mentioned in the previous chapter, an HID lighting system consists of a ballast, reflector, socket, and lamp (light bulb), and is intensely bright. HID lighting options for plant growth are typically metal halide (MH) or high-pressure sodium (HPS) systems. It is important to get an air-cooled system; the lights will last longer and will not heat the grow room as much. Some indoor growers with smaller grow rooms prefer the HPS 600 watt systems, as they produce less heat than 1,000 watt lamps and can be hung closer to the plants.

HASSLE-FREE TIP

The basic rule of thumb on lighting is 50 watts of HPS or MH light per square foot. Reflectors are popular for getting the most out of your lights, and many are designed for smaller growing areas. A completely self-contained design will be lightweight and usually includes hangers. Many are lined with a high-performance specular aluminum and come completely prewired.

To get a good idea on how many plants you can comfortably and healthily put into your space, measure the size of your final size containers, or better yet, lay the empty containers out in the grow room space. Many growers use drip pans under the containers to catch any water spillage, so allow space for drip pans if you plan to use them. Allow room for moving around and working on the plants.

Actually laying out the grow space with empty containers can save you a lot of work later on; it lets you walk through and revise your work flow requirements, and you can be realistic about how many plants are really possible in your available grow room space.

You will also have to study how your fans and lights will be placed. Do you have heavy ceiling beams to work with, or will you need to plan for and purchase light stands? Plan where to run venting and any refits needed to prevent light leakage to outdoors.

Always be extremely careful to install and use lighting systems properly; grow rooms can get hot very quickly, and you risk drying out or burning plants, not to mention the danger of fire from poorly installed or maintained equipment. Never have cords or outlets where water and electricity can mix.

HASSLE-FREE TIP

A best practice advised by experienced indoor growers is to always have a spare bulb at all times. The plants are very sensitive to changes in the light phases or photoperiods, and keeping them in darkness while you order another bulb is not the best for your plants' well-being.

Growing indoors is a far more technical experience than an outdoor grow. Currently, technologies are changing rapidly to respond to needs to cut power costs and reduce light heat while improving indoor plant performance. Many indoor growers are working with LEDs and T5 fluorescents for both these reasons. The best plan for an indoor grower just starting out is to know your space parameters, prepare the grow room properly, and do your research.

Before the indoor grower even starts a crop, a ventilation system also should be well thought out and already in place. For humidity control, cannabis grow rooms need a constant supply of fresh air in and old air out. Too much humidity will cause plants to stop growing.

Cannabis plants in their reproductive phase also emit a strong and distinctive odor that is eventually vented to the outside of your house or whatever building you use to grow in.

Transplanting on Schedule

The plants you are starting with will determine initially your transplanting schedule. Some propagators provide what is essentially a largish plant, two to three feet in height. Some provide a rooted clone, a tiny thing a few inches in size. You may be starting seedlings or rooting cuttings of your own.

If you are starting with a well-grown young female plant a few feet in height, transplant it at once into its largest, final container. It might as well get right to work at turning expensive soil and light into strong roots and healthy vegetative growth. Indoor plants rarely grow their central taproot very long or large; they instead rely on a healthy fine mass of almost hairlike side roots to pull in water and nutrients. A ground-planted cannabis plant can grow its central taproot as long as six feet, so this is a good example of how adaptable cannabis can be.

If you have a healthy clone with strong roots well started, again, go ahead and plant it in the final container for the same reasons as above; it will only go through any possible transplant shock one time and should surge along nicely.

You should plan on two to four weeks for cuttings to root and become actual little plant clones. Until then, keep their light relatively cool; fluorescent light is suitable. They need warmth, but not hot, bright light just yet.

If you have started from seed, and are not using feminized seed, you will be dealing with twice the amount of little plants than you want to end up with in your flowering phase. This is because cannabis is dioecious and must declare for the grower to know if the plant is male or female.

The first transplant for seedlings is usually from their little four-inch starter pots to a three- or five-gallon container. This will allow enough room for the plants to grow while they make their sexual determination. Unsexed seedlings can also be each allotted a two-gallon pot until they declare their sexual identities; this will not hurt them, though it may limit their final size. This is not necessarily a bad thing in an enclosed and finite space, and it has the added benefit of making it easier to move the males once you know which ones they are.

How to Transplant

Have the next size containers ready to go, filled partly with your prepared soil. Leave a hole a few inches deeper and wider than the transplants' current containers. You can check how much initial soil to put in the container by setting the plant in its existing pot inside and checking that you have left enough room for the incoming root ball.

Water the waiting soil, and stir to make certain it is uniformly dampened; check that the water drains well from the container. Scratch in a handful of bone meal; this will be easily accessible to the plant's roots and will aid in strong root production. Let the soil of the plants waiting for transplant get slightly dry; soil that is too wet will be heavy and has the potential to fall apart, breaking the root ball.

One person can easily perform early transplants. When the plants are taller and in heavy larger containers, you need a transplant-ing assistant to help you pull the pots. It will also be easier on you, particularly your back, to have a transplant pal. Remember, to get the plant out of the pot, you are going to be turning it over and using gravity to slide the root ball out. If you are not particularly strong or tall, a helper is essential. Root balls also do not always slide right out, and wrestling a heavy, earth-filled container while trying not to break the plant can get tricky and tiring.

HASSLE-FREE TIP

If you are using a helper, always make certain that you both understand the plan in advance—who is pulling the pot, and who is supporting and turning the plant. Otherwise, confusion can lead to broken plants or root balls. As soon as the pot-puller frees the root ball, he can quickly set the pot down and help support the root ball until it is settled gently into its new container.

Sometimes, despite all best efforts, a root ball will break. While this event is not ideal, do not panic; cannabis is a very strong plant. The plant will spend a little time adjusting its root growth and get back to strong vegetative growth; the root damage just puts it a little behind the schedule of its sisters.

Once the transplant is settled gently in place, fill in with your prepared soil and gently press around the plant's main stem with the flat palms of your hands. This will help bring the roots in contact with the soil. Water gently and press again to settle the plant. Make certain the plant's identifying label or tag is secured or written on the side of the container with indelible pen.

Lights and Your Transplants

Once you have your little plants transplanted, you will want your grow room lights to cycle for the vegetative phase. Make certain the plants get eighteen hour "days" and six hour "nights" for two full weeks. If you are using HID, place the young plants so they are twenty-four to thirty-six inches from the light source. If you have concerns about burning the plants, hold your own hand under the light where the tops of your plants will be; if it burns you, it will be burn them. You may need to adjust the light height up or down as you observe the plants. If they are getting "leggy," they are reaching too much, and the lights need to be lowered. Keep an eye on your lights. The plants are growing very rapidly, so be alert and prepared to adjust the height as often as needed.

If you are working with clones, they should be one to two feet tall by the seventh week in vegetative phase. At this time, you can change your light cycle to a twelve hour day and twelve hour night to induce flowering, or move the clones to a separate flowering room with this light cycle on timers. This is the time to switch to lower nitrogen and to feed for bloom.

Rotating Vegetative and Flowering Cycles

If you are working with seedlings, give an extra four weeks of growth in the vegetative phase before inducing flowering. This is where having separate vegetative and flowering rooms can give you more options. This setup also allows for continual cycling of vegetative and flowering plants. As soon as one crop is harvested and the flowering room deep cleaned, another group of vegetative plants can be installed and induced to flower. The vegetative room can also be cleaned and then will begin another cycle of young plants for a perpetual growing cycle.

Fertilizing for Vegetative Growth

Once your cuttings or seedlings are well started, the plants will enter their vegetative phase of growth. They are working at growing roots and gaining size, building strong stems and lots of healthy green leaves. During this phase the plants will need plenty of water and a great deal more nitrogen than during the flowering phase.

Organics rarely burn plants, but testing your soil and understanding the different properties of different organic amendments can, along with your budget, help you choose wisely. Packaged amendments generally list nitrogen, phosphorus, and potassium in that order.

Blood meal applications last up to four months and should be used with caution (outdoor growers use no more than four ounces per square yard during the growing or vegetative phase). Indoor growers are more likely to use it as an element in tea for their plants as dilution with water makes it less likely to burn tender young plants, and it is a good source of nitrogen.

As long as your plants are in a vegetative phase of growth, they will use a lot of nitrogen and push to grow big and leafy. Watch each plant as an individual, and feed a "power drink" of special compost or manure tea once a week. This can coincide with the plants' watering schedule for convenience.

Fertilizing for Flowering

As the plants start to flower, their vegetative growth will slow and then stop. The grower should stop feeding high nitrogen; the plants will need more phosphorus and potassium for flowering. If you are using premade organic supplements, look for a ratio of approximately 15-30-30 for flowering.

The plants will also need calcium, which you can supply by scratching finely ground organic eggshells into the soil around the main stem. An electric coffee grinder can be used to prepare the eggshells, but wear a mask as the fine powder is easy to inhale.

Water Requirements

Every indoor grow room should have a thermometer and a hygrometer installed because accurate measurements are essential for maintaining a healthy plant environment. Ideally you will use a thermometer that not only shows current temperature but records the high and low measurements for each day. This will give you valuable information as to how well your cooling and venting systems are working. The ideal temperature for an indoor grow is 72°F–76°F. The best range in relative humidity is from 60–70 percent for vegetative plants, dropping to 40–60 percent during the flowering phase.

The plants' water intake should be monitored daily, especially when they get bigger and use more water and have less room in their containers. If soil in the container is pulling away from the edge of the pot, it is time to water. The best time is when the soil is just starting to pull; otherwise, you will waste a lot of water that runs down between the pot and the root ball, and the plant might not be getting much at all.

Cannabis plants that are stressed for water will signal to you by leaf droop and a wilty look. They can bounce back very quickly, but stressing the plant over and over will take its toll. Do not let the plants dry out and beg for water, but ideally water deeply once a week.

Identifying the Peak Harvest Moment

At the end of the twelfth week in the indoor cycle, the plants should be ready, or nearly ready, for harvest. The grower must monitor trichomes at least daily to determine when to harvest. Generally, indoor growers, like outdoor growers, take their plants when the trichomes are just starting to turn amber.

Indoor growers have an advantage here by being able to control the growing environment. If they are working with a late-maturing strain or feel the flowering plants need another week of finish, they can choose to do so without worrying about the weather and potential crop loss to molds. A ripe cannabis flower will generally have both white and brown pistils showing from the third set as the trichomes are starting to turn from clear to amber. This is the ideal time to harvest.

Protection from Spider Mites

Almost nothing is more destructive to an indoor grow than a spider mite infestation; the crop and grower are both in for a bad time. If you see any indication of spider mites in your grow room, you must act immediately to protect your plants.

Spider mites, particularly the two-spotted spider mite (*Tetranychus urticae*) variety, are especially feared by the indoor cannabis grower. The spider mite is the most common and destructive of mite pests and will reproduce rapidly in hot conditions like a cannabis grow room. Mature female spider mites may produce a dozen eggs daily for a couple of weeks, so populations can increase with frightening rapidity. Spider mites are particularly dangerous for plants under water stress.

Spider mites live on the underside of leaves and puncture the plant's cells to feed. The first visible signs of infestation are light dots on the leaves. As the infestation advances, the leaves can take on a gray or bronze color. Then, the plant's leaves turn yellow and drop off. Your plant is signaling in every way it can that it is under attack and needs help. Leaves, twigs, and flowers become covered with large amounts of webbing, and the plants appear very sickly and stunted. As your plant's foliage declines in food value, female spider mites hitchhike onwards to other plants, and the cycle continues.

Spider Mite Features

Spider mites develop from eggs, which usually are laid near the veins of leaves during the growing season. After the eggs hatch, the old eggshells remain and can be useful in diagnosing spider mite problems. Check the underside of leaves for spider mites, their eggs, old eggshells, and the distinctive spider mite webbing. To the naked eye, spider mites look like tiny moving dots on the plant leaves. For a clear look at suspicious dots, examine your plants with a handheld lens with at least ten times (10x) magnification. The undersides of leaves are typically where spider mites start out living in webbed colonies containing hundreds of individual mites. Lightly misting your plants before spider mite inspections will make the webs much easier for you to see.

Preventative Measures

Make certain you do not unknowingly bring infested plants or carry mites on your clothes into contact with your grow room or any cannabis plant, whether indoor or outdoor.

Spider mites can live on plants other than cannabis, so any plants you handle or purchase should be inspected for spider mites, not just your cannabis. Never put new clones or plants in your main grow room without a period of isolation. Inspect them closely under magnification, and give a preventative bath with an organic insecticidal soap. The insecticidal soap kills the spider mites by compromising their cellular integrity; the spider mites are dissolved from the inside out.

Removing Spider Mites

Spider mites are happiest in hot, dryish conditions, with approximately 20–30 percent humidity. In temperatures above 80°F, spider mites can reproduce in as little as five days. For prevention during the vegetative phase of cannabis growth, periodic blasts with clean water can physically remove and kill many mites, as well as destroy the webbing where they lay their eggs. It is thought that spider mites may delay egg laying until new webbing is produced. Spraying flowering plants with water is not advised. The foliar drinking can slow resin production during the flowering phase, and too much moisture on colas can create an environment for mold.

You can also get rid of spider mites using your own insecticidal soap. Mix two or three drops of a liquid soap (such as Murphy Oil Soap or Ivory liquid) per quart of water and apply with a mister. Be sure to cover every inch of leaf, particularly the undersides where the mites live. Using a horticultural oil such as neem oil, an extract from the neem tree, is another alternative. Use neem oil during the day so that it will evaporate quickly and reduce the chance of damaging the plants.

Another treatment you can try is rubbing alcohol. Since it evaporates quickly there is little chance that it could harm the plants, but test spray a few leaves first to check the plant's reaction. For a strong mix, use a 1:1 ratio of alcohol to water, or if you want a gentler mix, try a 1:3 ratio of alcohol to water.

Treating yourself is also important, because if you find spider mites on new plants or clones, it means you can carry the spider mites along to your healthy plants. First treat the infested plants, then remove all of your clothing, bag it in plastic for removal to a washing machine, and immediately shower or bathe yourself. Do not forget to wash your hair.

Chemical Treatments

There are chemical controls (miticides and acaricides) for spider mites, but just because a chemical manufacturer advertises that a product kills spider mites does not mean this is a real solution. First of all, very few insecticides are effective for spider mites. Miticides do not affect the spider mite eggs, so you have to reapply every ten to fourteen days to control the hatching of eggs. This frequency of application creates resistant strains of spider mites and kills natural enemies like predatory mites, making long-term indoor control even more difficult for the grower.

Spider Mite Predators

The most useful predators of spider mites, and produced commercially for release as biological controls, are mites in the Phytoseiidae family. The Cornell University Extension office refers to *Phytoseiulus persimilis* as "one of the mainstays of greenhouse integrated pest management." Once the spider mites are gone, these predators feed on each other and eliminate their own populations.

When you are ordering mail order predators, generally figure that predatory mites should be placed out at a count of at least twenty per plant. The predators will not usually move from plant to plant, so they need to be placed in an even distribution by hand. Estimate how many to use based on the general idea that one predator mite can eat twenty spider mite eggs, or five adult spider mites per day.

Other Treatments

Moisture management is also an important cultural control for spider mites. Plants stressed by lack of water can produce changes in their chemistry that make them more appealing to spider mites. The indoor grower of cannabis has more control over how humid the grow environment is kept and should remember that spider mites need a fairly low humidity level to thrive.

Create sticky traps by smearing a resin like Tanglefoot on pot edges or cardboard that is an attractant color; spider mites appear to like yellow. Cardboard panels can be coated with Tanglefoot and placed on the walls. Periodically run your fans on high for about ten minutes. Users of this technique report the spider mites are blown off and stick on the Tanglefoot panel. You can also put Tanglefoot around air intakes; this can help trap incoming spider mites looking for a home. You will still need to treat the plants for eggs, but reducing the adult population will help you gain control.

Protection from Other Natural Pests

In addition to spider mites, there are other common cannabis predators. The grower should be on the lookout for signs of infestation and be prepared to tackle the problem.

Whitefly

Whitefly are quite small, approximately one-sixteenth of an inch long, and completely white. If you lightly shake the plant, they flutter around and then settle back. Whitefly suck on the juices in leaves, weakening plants and transferring disease from plant to plant.

French marigold (*T. patula*) is an annual that deters whiteflies, and it has roots that kill nonbeneficial nematodes. Marigolds in pots can be moved around the greenhouse or grow room. Make certain to get the specific variety *T. patula*, which is usually sold as French marigold.

Fungus Gnats

Fungus gnats can be problematic once they get a foothold in your grow room. They are spindly flies that look like tiny mosquitoes, with bodies about one-eighth of an inch long. The larvae live in the soil and cause the damage to plants, not the adults. Larvae are translucent gray to white, about one-quarter inch long, wormlike with no legs, and with shiny black heads. They can infest a crop from soil or algae under benches, from contaminated potting soil, or by adults flying short distances into the production area.

Larvae feed on decaying matter and on healthy and diseased roots in the soil medium; they are particularly damaging to seedlings or small clones. Fungus gnat problems result from overwet conditions and diseased roots; the alert grower will make haste to amend poor cultural conditions. Soils should be stored dry, and pots and production areas must be well drained. Fungus gnats need soil fungi, algae under benches, or a damp mossy place to get established.

Sometimes naturally occurring parasites can regulate fungus gnat populations, especially when broad-spectrum pesticides are not used in the production area. Fungus gnat parasites are much smaller than fungus gnats and look like fragile tiny wasps.

Adult fungus gnats are attracted to yellow sticky traps. Some growers also report that using diatomaceous earth (DE) on the topsoil of the pots is effective in killing fungus gnat larvae.

Molds

Botrytis is the most commonly seen mold in an indoor grow. It requires high humidity conditions (50 percent or higher) and some type of initial food source before it invades a healthy plant. Any debris from old leaves or bruised, broken plant parts can be enough to provide a food base, and eventually the fungus will invade healthy plant tissue and you will lose some, if not all, of your harvest.

Botrytis can initially be mistaken for a dusting of trichomes, but once in full bloom it presents as gray, almost hairlike, spots on the cola or flower, continuing rapidly to slimy, dark gray goo.

Prevention is the best cure; sanitation and good air circulation are the best weapons the grower has to prevent major botrytis or other mold outbreaks. Remove dead leaves or damaged tissue from the plants and keep the indoor grow room extremely clean. Do not throw dead leaves to the base of your plants; you will be creating a food source for botrytis and other pests.

Protection from Human Pests

Absolutely the most important thing you can do to protect your cannabis from theft is to not talk about it. This can be difficult, especially if your crop is beautiful, bountiful, and delicious. It is human nature to want to take credit for or to brag a little about your successful crop. You may be tempted to show your gorgeous grow to a trusted friend. If he has no "need to know," do not burden him with the responsibility of knowing about your crop.

Do not tell someone who asks where you got your wonderful cannabis. This can be someone you know well and trust implicitly, and may be trustworthy and would never mean harm to you, but again, there is human nature and the desire to talk. Bragging about knowing a really great grower is something that people sometimes do. They feel there is no harm in it because they are not giving your name.

The Impact of Law Enforcement

Another threat to consider is law enforcement—this depends on where you live and your legal status as a grower. In the right state, and the right counties within that state, law enforcement is not allowed to discriminate against licensed medical growers. It is sensible and right that a law-abiding citizen can call the police for help and get the same response as, for example, a cultivator of expensive bonsai who is being robbed would receive.

If you are illicitly growing indoors, instead of legally, your risk is greatly increased. The more people who know about your grow increases the chance that information about you will be traded to law enforcement by someone looking to improve his or her own legal situation. In other words, people will inform on others to reduce charges against themselves.

Landlords

If you rent your home, remember that there is one person who does have a right to access your living (and growing) quarters: your landlord. A landlord must give advance notice of a visit, either for a normal look around or perhaps to make some needed repair, but the landlord does own the property and has a right to inspect things. How you handle this depends on your own ethics, but in general, if you plan to grow anything larger than a closet grow, it is better to seek out a cannabis-friendly landlord and ask permission. Trying to dismantle a full-sized grow room in seventy-two hours (a typical advance notice time frame in most states) is tricky at best and of course raises the question of where to move it to.

CHAPTER NINE

CANNABIS OUTDOORS

Outdoor growers of cannabis have many trials and tribulations that the indoor grower never experiences. The outdoor grower will also enjoy some wonderful moments that the indoor grower misses out on by growing in controlled grow rooms. The time you spend outdoors with your plants will bring you much closer to nature.

The Advantages

In addition to the natural experience of outdoor gardening, there are other benefits to growing your cannabis outdoors. It will cost less, your yield should be larger and better tasting, and your carbon footprint will be smaller.

Less Expensive

Outdoor growing has the advantage of using the sun, air, wind, and rain—all of which are free. The plants can get larger planted in the ground and are generally healthier with less trouble and preventative labor associated with an inside grow. Soil improvement can take place on site instead of using only expensive bagged organic soils. A lot depends on the initial condition of your site's soil, but the more years you aerate, mulch, and add compost to a site, the better your soil will become. The garden repays you for your ongoing investment in time and materials each time you renew it.

> ↓ **LOW-CO$T TIP**
> Growing outdoors eliminates the need for artificial lights, fans, and humidity control devices as well as the power to operate them, the indoor growers' biggest expense.

If money is tight, you can plan ahead and improve your soil by mulching and composting with free materials. Leaves are everywhere in the fall and are excellent for improving soil. Many people bag their fall leaves for pickup by the city. Ask politely if you may take the bagged leaves instead; it saves labor for you, and the city homeowner is going to rake and bag the leaves anyway. Mulch your areas in the fall and till in the composted leaves in the spring. Rain-spoiled hay is usually available for free or very cheaply in rural areas; it holds down weeds in early spring and the composted hay improves soil very quickly.

The rural outdoor grower can gather manure for composting without offending the sensibilities of nearby neighbors. Goats, chickens, horses, and cows are usually nearby, and you can get wonderful nitrogen-rich compost makings for free.

Outdoor cultivation requires far less expensive equipment, electrical expertise, and labor. The plants still need to be regularly watered and fed, but most of their development will be accomplished simply by allowing them to grow over spring and summer.

Larger Yields

Outdoor plants generally yield more than indoor ones. This is simply because they are able to grow larger. Few indoor setups can accommodate plants as large as those grown outdoors. Assuming that detection is not a problem, outdoor plants can comfortably grow six to eight feet in height. It is fairly normal for plants of this size to produce a pound to a pound and a half of dried buds. Germinating seeds early in the growing season allow your plants a long vegetative period before flowering is triggered by the shorter days of late summer.

Better Taste

Many people prefer the taste and effect of organically grown cannabis and insist they can easily differentiate between cannabis grown with soil and sun and cannabis produced with hydroponics and grow lights.

Better for the Environment

The sun produces more light than any amount of metal halides together in one grow room. When comparing indoor to outdoor cannabis growing, there can be no doubt that growing cannabis by burning fossil fuels is less than earth friendly.

Indoor growers are frequently forced to spray chemicals for pest control or face losing their crop to spider mites. Not only does this encourage the development of pesticide-resistant pests, but there are health implications for the end users of the cannabis. The health issues are even more serious when the cannabis is grown for medical use; patients can be especially sensitive to chemical residues.

Materials

Unlike an indoor grow, outdoor growing only requires a little electricity at the beginning and for a few months at the end of the cycle when the crop is hanging and drying. Little seedlings are generally started indoors, partly to get a jump on the growing season, partly because it is easier to monitor them closely when they're handy, and partly to get them to a size where they are in less danger from natural predators like earwigs, pill bugs, slugs, and birds.

Starting

Starting outdoor plants indoors requires very little other than a warm and clear well-lighted workspace. They are not going to stay inside for very long—ten days at most. A seed-warming mat is very useful, but it's not really needed. Grow lights can be good, but new tender seedlings do fine with cool fluorescents and a side source for warmth. The grower needs seeds or clones; small starting pots; clean, lump-free soil; and clean water.

The Grow Area Outdoors

Some outdoor growers fence their cannabis, while others hide it by camouflage plantings. Both of these systems have advantages and disadvantages. Fencing needs to be high and of stout materials. This can get expensive and can alert potential thieves that you have something of value enclosed. Using camouflage is generally less expensive but can cost the grower his crop if casual trespassers, wildlife, or live-stock come across the crop and steal it or browse it to the ground.

Fencing has three functions: to screen your garden from casual observers, to keep out livestock and wild browsers like deer, and to keep out thieves. Thieves are the most difficult to prevent reaching your crop.

For optimized ripper protection, a grower can use a high board fence to minimize visibility, electric wire on the inside of the fence top to discourage climbers, and heavy gauge wire or stock panels around the plants. Add a large and noisy dog, and never leave the crop unguarded.

Containers

The grower who decides to grow plants in the ground will still need containers, especially if he grows from seed and must wait for sexual determination by the plants. It is far easier to control the male plants and pollen if you can simply pick up a container and move them into a closed environment away from your females.

A seedling should be grown in a protective container until it is two- to three-feet tall before placing it in the ground. The outdoor grower will need three- to five-gallon containers for each of the seed-lings during this interim phase.

Water

The outdoor grower must determine how to get water to the plants. This is generally achieved by sections of hosing. If you are growing in your backyard, this can mean a simple garden hose or two. If you are growing in a rural area and the crop is not near the water source, you can either haul it in or run potentially hundreds of feet of hose to the site, a definite expense. If you have long runs of hosing, remember that you should conceal or lightly bury it; visible hosing going into the brush or too far from a "normal" garden will alert thieves that you are growing cannabis. All they have to do is to follow the hose right to your crop.

Depending on the water source, an outdoor grower should factor in the costs of watering through a long, hot summer. Cannabis, particularly in the ground, uses a great deal of water, especially during the vegetative phase of growth. If your water has a bill attached to it (as opposed to having a well or spring), approximately $100 to $200 per month for three summer months is a reasonable estimate to water eighteen to twenty plants.

↓ LOW-CO$T TIP
You may find that it is easier and less expensive to run PVC piping to the grow site instead, but either way, bringing water to the crop is an expense to evaluate when you determine the grow site location.

Garden Tools

The outdoor grower's most valuable tool is a stout and well-made garden fork. You will use it for aerating soil, digging, and turning compost. You will also need a good long-handled shovel, a wheelbarrow, and a compost screener. Less essential, but useful and good to have, is a composter, especially if you live in a more urban area. Although a well-made compost pile should never smell, an enclosed composter will keep your composting activities inoffensive to neighbors. This has a side benefit of making them less likely to come over to your garden uninvited or to start peeking over the fence.

Some growers use a garden tiller. These can range in size from tiny eggbeaters that are useful for raised beds or starting plant site holes to riding tractors with big tiller attachments run by hydraulics.

Generally, heavy tilling of grow sites is a less than productive use of good soil. However, there are times when a tiller is very useful, especially when starting from unimproved soil or for incorporating tilth-building materials like spoiled hay or mushroom compost.

Tillers can be rented by the day; this is sometimes the best solution for the minimal use you will make of such an expensive machine. Also, remember, tillers run on gasoline or diesel, neither of which is inexpensive. If you do purchase or rent a tiller, figure on buying a few gas cans as well; you are going to have to transport and store fuel.

Soil Amendments

Soil amendments are another expense factor. These include potting soils, composts, minerals, and soils by the yard. Depending on the overall size of your crop, soil amendments can cost anywhere from a few hundred to a thousand dollars. Remember, you will also have to use fuel and time to procure soil supplies, and large amounts will require using a truck. As noted above, outdoor growers have the advantage of actually being able to build optimum soil. This takes time, however, and a first-year crop is going to need good soil immediately.

Drying

Once you are drying the crop, consider the expense for a dedicated building or drying room, purchasing fans and dehumidifiers, and the accompanying electrical bills to power them. You will also need heavy gauge wire and hardware to hang it, or racks for hanging the plants, as well as clean glass or plastic for storage after curing is completed.

The Soil

The basic requirement for cannabis is nutrient-rich, well-drained soil. A good starter mix is one-third sandy loam for drainage, one-third compost you have made, and one-third organic bagged soil.

You could just start out with organic bagged soil, as it usually contains sandy loam and is an excellent mix of other essentials, but it is very expensive. Using sandy loam is important for drainage and also for a slightly firmer soil texture. Sandy loam can be purchased in bulk at garden centers and by the yard in rural areas.

You can improve a reasonable soil with good organic gardening practices until you have ideal soil. Loam is the most desirable and is made up of 40 percent sand, 40 percent silt, and 20 percent clay. In this mix, the plant can access the good nutrients in clay soil because there is sufficient air available. When you are mixing your own soil, strive to create a similar blend to loam. Plant roots need air to access food, and while a dense, compacted soil like clay may have lots of nutrients, they remain unavailable to the plant due to lack of air. Good aeration also stimulates beneficial bacterial activity, allowing the plant to use more organic matter.

Soil Considerations

Compacted soil speeds up moisture loss; in hard, packed soils, water rises very rapidly to the surface and is lost through evaporation. This can lead to a much larger water bill than you initially anticipated for your grow.

The grower must also be alert to the acidity or alkalinity of the soil mix. Cannabis prefers a soil that is not too acid and not too alkaline; a pH of 6.5 is just about perfect. Some growers swear by a slightly lower pH; most estimate the range for soil-grown cannabis is 6.5 to 7.5.

Humus is important for improving water and nutrient-holding capacities. Humus contains complex organic compounds that remain after the many soil organisms have used and transformed the original material.

The Importance of Soil Dwellers

Living soil organisms decompose organic compounds, sequester nitrogen and other nutrients, and fix nitrogen from the atmosphere, making it available to the plants. Soil organisms interact with one another, with plants, and with the soil. The combined result is a number of beneficial functions including nutrient cycling, moderated water flow, and pest control.

This nutrient cycling and disease suppression is very complex and very much needed for a healthy garden. Dead, chemically treated soils are bad for the environment as well as nonconductive to good plant health and natural disease controls. The wise outdoor grower will work with nature and encourage natural controls.

Choosing the Right Strains

Cannabis breeders have spent years modifying plant characteristics to optimize quality and production. Information about their observation and genetic manipulation is available either through books or on the web, so learning where strains are typically grown can give you your first clue as to what might improve your growing success.

The Classics

Some strains remain classics and are available for years. Others are improved upon and become harder to find as growers prefer the upgraded version. Northern Lights, Big Bud, and White Widow are considered classics. These are strains that have survived the test of time and are readily available via online seed sites.

The best seed sites will list their strains like a good garden catalog; they list provenance, typical characteristics of the strain in appearance, preferred growing conditions, and the qualities of the end product, usually both for productivity and effects. This is very useful if you plan to breed and fine-tune a strain of your own that is ideally suited to your tastes and your particular microclimate.

Location Matters

Outdoor plants need an environment to which they are genetically predisposed. Pure sativa strains that do well in California or in the southern parts of the United States do not finish as well in the shorter growing seasons farther north.

The northern parts of the United States can be considered quite a cold climate. The outdoor grower in this region should use strains specifically bred for colder climates. These are mostly indica or indica/sativa mixes. Some of these strains are commercially available, like a Northern Lights crossed with Big Bud or White Widow. It is important to have strains that can finish in the shorter northern growing season.

The southern part of the United States is a mild and warm climate, and many strains can be grown outdoors in this region. Pure indica, pure sativa, and hybrid strains can all be used. Pure sativas particularly like long growing seasons and lots of warmth.

Special Considerations

Due to the outdoor cycle's long growing period and chances of rain soaking the plant near harvest time, a plant with a treelike structure is more suited to an outdoor grow. Its air circulation is better than a super-bushy, dense structure that is more prone to molds if the leaves get wet.

If you are acquiring cloned strains from an indoor grower, and they are commercially available as well, it is worthwhile to look up online to see how it performs outdoors. A clone raised outdoors may perform differently than its mother grown indoors.

The Growing Cycle (Brief)

The outdoor grower must determine when spring really starts in the area where she lives. California growers have one of the best climates in the country for growing outdoor cannabis; they can get their seedlings out early and grow massive sativas without fear that the plants will not finish in time. Other parts of the United States have a long, cool, rainy spring season, and the farther north the area, the shorter the growing season.

Starting the Cycle

The cycle starts when you procure clones or start your seeds. These little ones will need to be nurtured until they reach a safe size to be put outdoors. Remember, clones do not have to be the size of a cutting; this is just when growers generally receive them from the propagator. Clones can arrive sometimes as three- or four-foot tall plants. The downside is that this larger clone is probably root bound and will experience difficulties as it tries to adjust to real sunlight. The sun is far more powerful than grow lights, and it takes them a little while to adjust.

The Vegetative Phase

The first transplant for seedlings is usually from their little four-inch starter pots to a three- or five-gallon container. This will allow enough room for the plants to grow while they make their sexual determination.

Once the plants are in their container they will enter their vegetative phase of growth where they grow roots and gain size as well as build strong stems and lots of healthy green leaves. During the vegetative phase, the plants will need plenty of water and more nitrogen than during the flowering phase. Cannabis is light sensitive and requires a light trigger to begin the phase of flower development so desired by cannabis growers.

If the grower plans to make clones from this crop, now is the time to take cuttings. It is possible to clone from a flowering plant, but this is not advised. It takes the cutting far longer to root, and the new little plant may try to flower right away. An eight-inch flowering plant is really not of much use or desirable in any way.

Transition to Flowering Phase

The plants will grow until daylight shortens to twelve hours. This is the sign or trigger to the plants to begin flowering. The days remaining for reproduction are dwindling, and the plants will strive to complete the flowering and seeding stages, which is their natural goal.

If the grower plans to breed for seed, he will have isolated a male or males of preferred lineage and collected and labeled their pollens. As soon as the female plants show pistils, the grower can pollinate selected branches to create new hybrids and fresh seed for next year. The grower can continue to breed the females until harvest time, but late breedings will not give the plants enough time to produce mature and viable seeds.

As the plants grow flowers, their vegetative growth will slow and then stop. They are concentrated on reproduction, and a large array of healthy, resin-covered flowers is their natural way to catch wind-borne pollen. The grower has mostly frustrated this goal by removing the males and selectively breeding, but the plants will not know this and produce resins as fast as they can. At this time, stop feeding nitrogen and increase the ratio of phosphorus and potassium that the plants need for flowering.

During this phase, the careful grower spends quite a bit of time grooming the plants by removing yellowed leaves and clearing any plant debris that falls to the ground. This will decrease pest infestations and is essential in preventing different molds that effect cannabis plants (and particularly the flowers).

The End of the Cycle to Harvest

Different hybrids and even different plants within a strain will complete their flowering at different times. Some strains finish as early as early September, while others, typically sativa types, take weeks longer to maximize resin production and finish. Sometimes the outdoor grower is forced to take the late finishers in to hang a little sooner than he would like. This is a trade-off: leaving the plants out can sometimes improve the quality of the finished product, but a rainy fall and late harvest leads to mold and the subsequent loss of buds.

Harvesting Outdoor Plants

If you love and grow cannabis, there is probably nothing more fun than harvesting a healthy, gorgeous outdoor plant. Not all of the plants will come in at once; this is an advantage of the outdoor grow, as indoor growers generally take all their plants at once and must process them at once, too.

As the flowers mature, the grower is watching the trichomes closely. Some growers like to take the plants while the trichomes are still clear. There is some indication that the clearer trichomes produce more of a psychoactive effect. Other growers wait until the trichomes are just starting to turn toward amber in color; they claim

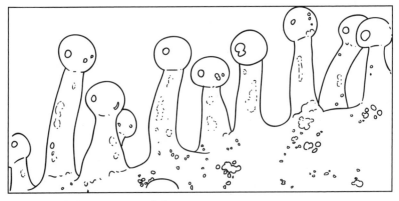

Enlarged image of trichomes (resin) on a cannabis flower.

this produces more of a "stony" effect. A lot of the effects are due to genetics, but it is definitely important to not let the trichomes go dark amber; the plant resins are starting to deteriorate at this point and heading in the direction of diminishing returns.

HASSLE-FREE TIP

Even if you grow legally, it is usually wise to take plants in when it is dusk or at some point when you will not be easily observed. It is very possible that someone, like a ripper, has been watching you to see when the plants are ready. If you harvest one or two, that is a signal to the rippers to come in and clear your crop site.

Harvesting Essentials

Generally it is easier to have a helper when you harvest large outdoor plants. One person can hold and steady the plant while the other cuts the trunk. Have a clean tarp lying open to lay the plant on; you do not want any dirt in your lovely colas. If the plants are wet, shake as much moisture out as possible.

Some plants are so large it makes sense to cut them in sections. This is fine as long as you have labels for each section. Always remove the labeled seed branch and hang it in a special spot just for your seeders; this way you will not lose track of it, which is easy to do with a largish crop.

Once your plants are safely indoors and hanging to dry, you still have to keep monitoring and acting decisively if you spot mold. Also be sure to keep your drying shed locked and preferably monitored twenty-four hours a day until the harvest is dried and manicured.

After-Harvest Instructions

After the harvest is completed, the good outdoor grower goes out into the site and does some clean up and preparation for next year by removing old cannabis leaves that might encourage pests, pulling old root balls, and layering compost materials over the in-ground spots to mellow through the winter.

The outdoor grow has one more advantage, and it only happens once a year. The outdoor grower, like any farmer, gets a winter break.

CHAPTER TEN

THE GROWING CYCLE (OUTDOORS)

Outdoor growers tend to have a much longer relationship with individual plants, unlike the indoor grower who has a twelve-week cycle. This long-term interaction often generates true affection for each plant as a living entity, especially if the growers are working with small crops of ten to twenty plants. First-time growers of outdoor cannabis will have a far greater chance of success if they do their homework first, and also prepare for several months of activity. That being said, just like any other gardening activity, growing cannabis outdoors in a low-key, casual manner can result in a fairly bountiful crop. Nature is going to help you, and the characteristics of cannabis will help you, too.

Understanding Nature's Schedule

Cannabis is a plant that craves warmth. Depending on where you live, the return of sunlight and warmth in the spring can be as early as the end of March or as late as mid-June. Trying to germinate seed or transplanting to an outdoor site when the temperatures are still wintery is a waste of time and potential plants.

The best way for a first-time outdoor grower to find out when to start is to contact the local Extension Service. These are usually state-funded agricultural information resources, but a quick look at your county government listings should supply a phone number or website address. Obviously, you will not ask about proper timing for planting cannabis, but inquiring about tomatoes will elicit the information you need. The Extension Service records information like local dates for the last and first frosts, as well as rainfall averages for different micro-climates. This information will be very useful to you as you plan your schedule for the outdoor grow.

Many outdoor growers start their plants indoors and have them already well grown and ready for hardening off and outdoor transplant. The outdoor grower wants as much time for vegetative growth as possible; once the sunlight drops to twelve hours, your plants will slow and then stop increasing in size, and begin to con-centrate on producing flowers. Unlike the indoor grower, you have no control over this timing. The female cannabis plant's hard-wired ultimate goal is to reproduce through pollination, so it will focus every bit of its energy on this very important activity. The grower benefits by frustrating the plant's desire by withholding access to male pollen.

Transplanting on Schedule

Any seedling going in the ground should be strong and tall enough to do so safely. Until they are at least two to three feet in height, they need containers to protect them. This is also about the size at which cannabis normally shows its sexual identity. Until they sex, you should not plant undifferentiated seedlings in the ground or their final large container. It becomes too hard to move the males, and it takes a lot of work and expensive materials to prepare a final plant site.

The outdoor grower should plan on needing three-gallon and five-gallon containers for each of the seedlings' interim phase. The rooted cuttings, or clones, should also be allowed to reach two to three feet for ground planting. If you are growing them full cycle in a large container, go ahead and plant or "bump" them right away; you know they are females and you can encourage vigorous vegetative growth right away. The clones will not have to experience more than one transplant shock; seedlings go through one or two. This can be so minimal that the plants probably are not even aware that they have been replanted.

Preparing to Transplant

When you get ready to transplant, always have everything ready to go. The goal is to minimize any shock or damage to the plants; otherwise, they lose valuable time recovering and adjusting themselves, meaning loss of size and productivity.

You will need:

- The container, washed and clean, or the ground site prepared and lined with chicken wire for each plant to be transplanted
- Prepared soil, screened and amended with compost and minerals
- Bone meal
- Water

- Sharpie pen for writing on containers, or premade labels for each plant
- Young plant to be transplanted

Plan to transplant in the cool of the evening; this gives the plants a cool, dark period to adjust to their new homes. If you must transplant during the day, try to get it done in the early morning before the sun gets high and hot.

Water the waiting soil and stir to make certain it is uniformly dampened, and check that the water is draining from the container well. Make a hole a few inches deeper and wider than the transplants' current containers, and scratch in a handful of bone meal. This will be easily accessible to the plants' roots and will aid in strong root production.

Transplant Assistants

One person can easily perform early transplants. Once the plants get three feet or more, or are in heavy five-gallon containers, it is much easier and also safer for the plants to have a transplanting assistant. Remember, to get the plant out of the pot, you are going to be turning it over and using gravity to slide the root ball out. If you are not particularly tall, a tall helper is essential. Root balls also do not always slide right out, and wrestling a heavy, earth-filled container while trying not to break the plant can get tricky.

As soon as the pot-puller frees the root ball, he can quickly set the pot down and help support the root ball until it is settled gently into its new container or the ground site. It is usually a good idea to bring the plants awaiting transplant to their ground site or the larger containers one at a time. Pot-pullers can get excited and fling an empty container as they jump forward to help support the root ball; unfortunately, if they fling blindly, a waiting plant can get broken.

Finalizing the Transplant

Once the transplant is settled gently in place, fill in with more of your prepared soil and gently press around the plant's main stem with the palms of your hands flat. This will help bring the roots in contact with the soil. Water gently and press again to settle the plant. Make certain the plant's identifying label or tag is secured or written on the side of the container with indelible pen. Now you are finished and can start on the next one.

Sexing Male and Female Plants

Cannabis from seed starts out with no visible sexual differentiation at all. The main concern is to provide them with light, water, and plenty of food for strong roots and healthy vegetative growth until they sex or "declare." At this point, all your seedlings can stay together, although you need to think through which genetic traits are the most important to you, how many males you want, and where to put them once they declare. They will have to be moved quickly once they provide proof of their sexual determination.

The male and female cannabis plants have very different-looking flowers that develop from a tiny nub, known as the "primordia," located initially on the main stems. The best place to check for flowering is at the top of the plant at the nodes (or intersections) where the plant develops a small leaf spur. The initial primordia will appear behind this spur and will start out looking like a tiny rounded pod.

Eventually the primordia either elongates into a tubular looking female calyx or the more rounded nubbin of the developing male flower. The easiest way to sex cannabis plants is to wait for two white hairs or "pistils" that will appear from the end of the female calyx. These pistils can also appear pinkish or yellowish, but they are very clear declarations that the plant is female.

HASSLE-FREE TIP

A novice grower can avoid some anxiety by asking an experienced grower to show him the first pistils, but if this resource is not available to you, do not worry. You know what you are waiting for, and when you see it for the first time it will be clear.

Remember that the plants will spend a fair amount of time over this process; it is not necessary to identify sexual determination and act within hours. You can keep watching for days until there is a clear and unambiguous display of the pistils.

Once your plants have declared, you must remove the males to their isolated, enclosed space to wait for pollen production. Make certain the males will be indoors where they can be severely segregated; absolutely no random pollen transfer should be possible.

As soon as you have collected pollen, you can breed selected branches on the females you choose to breed. There is no reason to wait until the female makes big flowers; pollination and fertilization can take place as soon as the pistils are displayed. Breeding early on also allows time for seed to mature; breeding later in the season can result in pale, whitish-green, immature seeds that are not likely to be viable.

Fertilizing for Vegetative Growth

Different organic soil amendments are usually needed when you are starting a grow site. Testing your soil and understanding the different properties of different organic amendments can, along with your budget, help you choose wisely. Packaged amendments generally list nitrogen, phosphorus, and potassium in that order. Always check, as extremely high nitrogen can burn plants.

Blood meal applications last up to four months and should be used with caution. Use no more than four ounces per square yard during the growing or vegetative phase. Growers do use it as an element in tea for their plants, and dilution with water makes it less likely to burn tender young plants.

As long as your plants are in a vegetative phase of growth, they will use a lot of nitrogen and push to grow big and leafy. Watch each plant as an individual, particularly if ground planted, and feed a "power drink" of special compost or manure tea once a week. This can coincide with the plants' watering schedule for convenience.

Fertilizing for Flowering

Once cannabis begins its flowering phase, you should stop any foliar feeding. Flowering cannabis plants secrete resins for more than one reason, but note that resins are a natural insulation from the elements. Foliar feeding in the flowering phase cools the plants and causes less resin secretion. Foliar feeding should only be done in the vegetative phase, and it should be stopped within two weeks after flowering begins.

Stop all feedings for two weeks before harvesting your plants, giving only water if needed. In many areas the grower will already be struggling with the beginning of fall rains and probably will not need to water at all.

As cannabis begins flowering, the plants will need more phosphorus and potassium than during the vegetative phase of growth. They will still need some nitrogen, but not as much as they did during vegetative growth. They also need calcium, which you can supply by scratching finely powdered organic eggshells into the soil around the main stem. If you are using premade organic supplements, look for an N-P-K ratio in the neighborhood of 15-30-30 for flowering.

Compost and Manure Teas

Organic fertilizers of any kind are beneficial to any soil. They build up the organic content of the soil, which improves its drainage and structure. By improving soil structure, you increase its ability to hold and release nutrients. The natural breakdown of the organic material by beneficial soil organisms can provide almost all the nutrients that a plant requires during the vegetative and flowering phases.

The Importance of Compost Tea

Although it should only be used as a foliar spray (or, in other words, sprayed on leaves) during the vegetative phase of cannabis, compost tea helps suppress foliar diseases, increases the amount of nutrients available to the plant, and speeds the breakdown of toxins. If you only apply compost to your soil in the traditional way, you can miss out on additional benefits from compost.

↓ LOW-CO$T TIP
Why make a compost tea rather than just working compost into the soil? Compost tea will make the benefits of compost go farther. And it has many benefits.

Compost extract (unlike compost tea) is a watery extract made from compost suspended in a barrel of water for no more than one hour before use, soaking in an old pillowcase or burlap sack. The benefit of extract is a supply of soluble nutrients that can be used as a gentle liquid fertilizer. This method is good for a quick mix but lacks sufficient holding time for beneficial microorganisms to multiply and grow significantly.

Compost teas are different from compost extracts—they are brewed much longer with microbial food and catalyst sources added to the solution, ideally a bubbler aerating the solution with oxygen. The aim of the brewing process is to extract beneficial microbes from the compost itself, followed by growing these populations of microbes during the twenty-four to thirty-six hour brewing period. The compost provides the source of microbes, and the microbial food and catalyst amendments promote the growth and multiplication of microbes in the tea. Microbial food sources can include molasses, kelp powder, and fish powder. Some examples of microbial catalysts are humic acid, yucca extract, and rock dust.

Manure Teas

Manure tea is a term used almost interchangeably with compost tea, and it is made and used in the same way. It is still required that the manure be composted, but it is pure composted manure as opposed to the blend of materials used for compost. Some people like to use chicken manure, while some prefer manure from steer or horses; others even recommend exotic manures from the local zoo. Generally, poultry manure is highest in nitrogen content, followed by hog, steer, sheep, cow, and horse manure.

Bat guano, or bat feces, is expensive manure, but it contains so many necessary macro- and micronutrients, as well as beneficial microorganisms, that it is very highly prized by cannabis gardeners. Guano from insect-eating bats is very high in nitrogen; fruit-eating bats produce guano that is higher in phosphorus.

Guano generally consists of ammonia, along with uric, phosphoric, oxalic, and carbonic acids, plus some earth salts and a high concentration of nitrates. Guano supplies nutrients in these approximate amounts: 9 percent nitrogen, 6 percent phosphorus, and 2 percent potassium.

All manures used in making manure tea should be well composted. The heat generated by composting will kill unwanted seeds and possible pathogens.

Water Requirements

Watering outdoor cannabis, particularly plants grown in containers, can be a little tricky. You must learn to observe the plants closely, as you are dealing with individuals, and pay attention to the weather variations that are part of an outdoor grow. Although large cannabis plants outdoors prefer a deep, once-a-week soaking, high temperatures and drying winds can speed up their need for water. Do not feel like you must stick to a rigid watering schedule. If the plants are thirsty and stressed two days before their scheduled watering, the attentive cannabis gardener will water right away.

As a general rule, let the plants dry out slightly between waterings; you want their roots to reach or stretch a little bit. Cannabis is also very resentful of soggy soil; it can create a very unhealthy environment that is too full of ammonia and that lacks air, something very essential for healthy roots and good plant growth.

If your plants are in large containers, the soil should be dry enough to just be starting to pull away from the edge of the container before you water again. The best way for you to check on the moisture level in your plants' soil is to put your finger down in the soil and feel. Dew can make the top layer of soil look quite moist, but the finger test can show if soil is bone dry a few inches below and if the plants need water.

Ground-planted plants need a slow drip that, depending on your soil, can be left on them for hours. When water starts to pool around the plant's base, move the drip to the next plant. Plants in large containers should also have slow watering; this gives the water a chance to soak down through all of the soil. Trying to water quickly will just create channels of least resistance, and possibly damage side roots. As a general rule, water container plants so that the water pools and drains three times in the session.

How to Field Groom and Identify Harvest Time

Once the plants start into their flowering phase, there will be a natural yellowing and drop of fan leaves. If this occurs before flowering begins, the cannabis gardener has cause for concern. This usually means a lack of nitrogen or other soil imbalance, and the grower should immediately test the soil for pH and N-P-K. Sometimes, excessive yellowing indicates that the plant has too much nitrogen, especially if it has been overfed. It is always important to test before trying to adjust soil values.

The natural yellowing and leaf drop is a good sign that things are proceeding as nature intended, but the good cannabis grower needs to start grooming her plants. Clumps of dead leaves that catch in the plant stems or surround the main stem on the ground are just breeding areas for molds and pests. The flowers need all the air circulation they can get, so you must help your plants by removing dying fan leaves on a daily basis. This is actually a very pleasant activity and beneficial in that it requires the grower to closely examine each plant every day. This close contact will ensure that you spot any pest problems or developing molds right away.

Gently flex yellowed leaves near the stem; if they are ready, they will pop right off. Do not tear or pull hard on the leaves. Some plants will drop far more leaves than other types; this has to do with their individual natures. Always take leaf debris away from the grow site; this keeps the garden area cleaner and less likely to provide breeding areas for pests.

It is not uncommon to see plants that are almost completely naked of fan leaves from natural drop and others cling to their leaves pretty much all the way into harvest. The grower should note this characteristic in her grow book; leaves that do not fall will have to be clipped later on, making more work during the processing phase of cannabis production.

Once the plants are dropping leaves and the flowers are producing trichomes as fast as they can, the grower must monitor each plant daily for the best harvest timing. Generally, growers take their plants when the trichomes are just starting to turn amber. Another way to estimate the length of time to harvest is to note the pistil "sets." The flower, or cola, will push out a first set of pistils that will brown. This is normal. It then produces a second set, they brown, and then on to the third set. A ripe cannabis flower will generally have both white and brown pistils showing from the third set as the trichomes are starting to turn from clear to amber. This is the ideal time to harvest.

Companion Plantings and Plant Protection from Natural Pests

Cannabis is quite clever at producing its own insect-repelling qualities. It is mainly when the cannabis plants are stressed that insects like leafhoppers move in. It is thought that the stressed plant emits a pheromone that the insects pick up on and they then start attacking the weakened plant. The sudden appearance of insect pests can actually mean your plant is signaling you that it is stressed for water or some other basic need.

Part of growing cannabis outdoors is working with nature, and using natural insect and pest controls is part of this program. You can create a balanced and healthy garden by interspersing what are called "companion" plants amongst the cannabis grow. These are plants that have many and varied benefits and attributes. Some of these plants attract beneficial insects or birds, some of these plants are actual repellants for pests, and some of these plants are contact irritants or poisons.

HASSLE-FREE TIP
It is always much easier to prevent a problem than to fix it later. By including companion plants in your garden, you can prevent or reduce infestations of many damaging insect pests.

Some of the more common and useful companion plants available to American growers for pest control include:

- Sunflowers are thought to be the number one trap plant for sucking, rasping insects like grasshoppers, leafhoppers, and aphids. These pests seldom damage the sunflowers. It is amazing to see leafhoppers congregating on sunflowers only feet away from your cannabis plants; the cannabis, especially when healthy and flowering, is a far less attractive option for the leafhopper. Sunflowers are an annual and are very easy to grow; one small packet of seed will provide plenty of trap plants, as well as tall camouflage cover for your growing cannabis. You can harvest the sunflower seeds for birdseed, and to plant for sunflowers next spring. Sunflowers also attract hummingbirds, which in addition to feeding on flower nectars, eat ants, mosquitoes, aphids, gnats, midges, caterpillars, flying ants, weevils, small beetles, whitefly, and insect eggs.
- French marigold (*T. patula*) is an annual that deters whiteflies and has roots that kill nonbeneficial nematodes. Ground

plant these marigolds around outdoor cannabis. Marigolds in pots can be used in greenhouses as well. Make certain to get the specific variety *T. patula*, which is usually sold as French marigold.

- Anise is a tender annual herb that grows from one to two feet in height. It is considered a good host for wasps that prey on aphids, and it is also said to repel aphids.
- Chives are perennials and keep aphids away. Chives are thought to repel Japanese beetles as well. A tea made from chives is sometimes used to protect against downy and powdery mildews. A side benefit of growing chives as companion plantings is that it's an excellent culinary herb.
- Coriander, also known as cilantro, is an annual culinary herb commonly used in Chinese and Mexican recipes. Coriander is known to repel aphids and spider mites. A tea made from coriander can be used as an organic spray for spider mites.
- Yarrow is an attractive flowering perennial herb that grows fairly tall; its feathery foliage can reach up to three feet or more. Yarrow has insect repelling qualities and is an excellent natural fertilizer.
- Catnip is a perennial member of the mint family. It deters flea beetles, aphids, Japanese beetles, squash bugs, ants, and weevils. Some growers report that it repels mice and voles as well. As with any mint, be careful it does not take over your garden; it is advisable to plant in containers to keep it under control.
- Clover is useful as a green manure, and it fixes nitrogen in the soil. It attracts many beneficial insects like aphid predators.
- Four o'clocks, or *Nicotiana*, is a tall annual that is quite poisonous and is not recommended around small children. It will attract and kill Japanese beetles, which feed on the foliage and

then die very rapidly. The flowers open in the evening (hence the common name of "four o'clocks") and have a strong scent reminiscent of the suntan oils of the 1960s.

- Geraniums are an edible annual that will repel cabbageworms and Japanese beetles. They also are a trap plant for leafhoppers.

- Gopher purge, or *Euphorbia lathyris*, is also sometime known as mole plant. It is a biennial plant (lives for two years) that contains milky sap that is found in the roots, leaves, and flowers. This is a caustic substance that is not a repellant but a contact irritant; the animal must chew the roots to become ill or die. A thick stand of *E. lathyris* planted in the gopher's main tunnel is necessary to protect plants, as you want a preventative effect.

- Horehound (*Marrubium vulgare*) is a sturdy perennial member of the mint family. Its many tiny flowers attract Braconid and Icheumonid wasps, and Tachnid and Syrid flies. The larval forms of these insects parasitize or otherwise consume many other insect pests. It blooms over a long season, continually attracting beneficial insects, an excellent attribute for a companion plant. It is said to stimulate and aid in fruiting in tomatoes and peppers.

- Lavender is a strongly scented, tall-growing perennial herb. It comes in many varieties and colors and is known to repel whitefly, fleas, and codling moths. Lavender also nourishes many nectar-feeding and beneficial insects. Plants can be started in winter from cuttings, to be planted out in spring.

- Peppermint is another perennial member of the mint family. Its high menthol content acts as a repellant for white cabbage moths, aphids, and flea beetles. It is an attractant for bees and other beneficial insects. As with other mints, keep watch that it does not take over your entire garden. Peppermint will do fine in containers, which can be moved around as needed for aphid control.

- Petunias are an inexpensive and pretty flowering annual. They repel the asparagus beetle, leafhoppers, certain aphids, tomato worms, Mexican bean beetles, and general garden pests. The leaves can also be used in a tea to make a potent bug spray.
- Sweet alyssum is a self-seeding annual that is another natural control for aphids. Alyssum flowers attract hoverflies whose larvae devour aphids. They will reseed freely and make a beautiful groundcover every year.

Diatomaceous Earth (DE)

Diatomaceous earth is the finely ground fossils of prehistoric freshwater diatoms: tiny, single-celled algae found in plankton. DE is a fine, white, crystalline powder that is perfectly safe for humans and other mammals but deadly for garden pests. The abrasive quality of diatomaceous earth scrapes the protective outer shell off of insects. Without this protective layer, insects die very rapidly. A protective dusting of diatomaceous earth around plants will kill many insects, including slugs and fungus gnats. DE is considered a good organic gardening practice and is found at most garden centers. It kills insects, slugs, and snails within forty-eight hours of contact. Because DE is a contact irritant, use it to deplete pest populations, but still protect plants from slugs and snails by hand picking at night.

Wood Ash

Clean wood ash sprinkled around the perimeter area of a garden will deter slugs and snails, as well as supplying beneficial potash to the soil. Always make certain the ash is from a clean burn, meaning no colored papers, plastics, or other household debris is in the ash. Dyes and plastics can add toxins to your soil.

Protection from Human Pests

Another use of companion plantings is for camouflage for your cannabis. Tall annuals like dill, fennel, corn, and hops vines grow very rapidly and will help screen your plants from prying eyes.

Blackberry Maze

Some rural growers make tunnels through tall blackberry growth and create small clearings for their cannabis plants. This is quite labor intensive, and frequently painful, as thorny blackberry does not give up without a fight. You will also have to pack all your soil and containers into each individual clearing, as well as plan a way to get water to the hidden plants. Hosing must be covered and hidden from aerial view; otherwise, you are creating virtual signposts right to the location where the plants are hidden.

Fencing and Camouflage

Some outdoor growers fence their cannabis, while others hide it by camouflage plantings. Both of these systems have advantages and disadvantages. Fencing needs to be high and of stout materials. This can get expensive and can alert potential thieves that you have something of value enclosed. Using camouflage is generally less expensive but can cost the grower her crop if casual trespassers, wildlife, or livestock come across the crop and steal it or browse it to the ground.

Timing Is Important

Even if you grow legally, it is usually wise to take plants in when it is dusk or at some point when you will not be easily observed. It is very possible that someone, like a ripper, has been watching you to see when the plants are ready.

CHAPTER ELEVEN

DEALING WITH MITES

Outdoor growers may deal with many more variables than the indoor grower, who, after all, can control light, water, wind, and humidity levels, but generally they do not have to battle spider mites. On the other hand, nothing strikes greater terror in the indoor grower than a spider mite infestation, which can lay siege to an entire crop.

What Are Mites?

Spider mites, predominantly the two-spotted spider mite (*Tetranychus urticae*) variety, are extremely destructive pests that mostly attack indoor cannabis grows. Although they are related to insects, spider mites are members of the arachnid class along with spiders and ticks. Spider mites are sometimes called web-spinning mites and are the most common and destructive of mite pests. If you even suspect you have spider mites in your grow room, you must act quickly to protect your plants.

Spider mites reproduce rapidly in hot conditions like those found in a cannabis grow room; a generation can be completed in less than a week. After mating, mature females may produce a dozen eggs daily for a couple of weeks, leading to extremely rapid increases in spider mite populations. Plants under water stress are highly susceptible. As the food quality of your plant's foliage declines, female spider mites hitchhike onwards to other plants, and the cycle continues.

What Do Mites Look Like?

Depending on your age and vision quality, to the naked eye, spider mites look like tiny moving dots on the plant leaves. They are so tiny that an initial infestation is easy to miss until you start seeing damage to the plants. For a clear look at suspicious dots, it is more efficient to examine your plants with a handheld lens with at least ten times magnification.

You are looking for adults and eggs. The adult spider mites have eight legs and an oval body, with two red eyespots near the head end of the body. Adult females, which are the largest, are less than a twentieth of an inch long. Females usually have a large, dark blotch on each side of the

Spider mite.

body and numerous bristles covering the legs and body. The immature spider mites resemble the adults, except the newly hatched larvae have only six legs.

HASSLE-FREE TIP

If you spot what you think are spider mites, shake a few off the leaf onto a white sheet of paper. Once you disturb them, they will move around rapidly.

Spider mites develop from eggs, which usually are laid near the veins of leaves during the growing season. Most spider mite eggs are round and extremely large in proportion to the size of the mother. Spider mite eggs are spherical and translucent; they look like tiny droplets of water that become cream colored just before hatching. After the eggs hatch, the old eggshells remain and can be useful in diagnosing spider mite problems. Check the underside of leaves for spider mites, their eggs, old eggshells, and the distinctive spider mite webbing.

An infested plant. Note that webs are like what a spider makes, but these are mites.

Spider mites live in colonies frequently containing hundreds of individual mites that generally appear on the undersurfaces of leaves. The name "spider mite" probably comes from the silk webbing typically produced on infested leaves. The presence of this webbing is the easiest way to distinguish them from other types of mites. Lightly misting your plants before inspecting them will make the webs much easier to see.

Remember, you are looking for a very tiny spider-like creature, usually appearing in colonies; make sure that you do not destroy beneficial small garden spiders, usually those operating as helpful individuals, as it is sometimes easy to confuse their small useful webs with spider mite webbing.

Plant Indicators of Infestation

Spider mites cause damage by sucking cell contents from the plant's leaves. Injury is caused as they feed, bruising the cells with their small, whiplike mouthparts and ingesting the sap. An infestation level high enough to show visible damage to leaves can be very destructive. The first visible signs of infestation show up as a stippling of light dots on the leaves; sometimes the leaves take on a sickly gray or bronze color. As the infestation continues, the plant's leaves turn yellow and drop off. Leaves, twigs, and flowers become covered with large amounts of webbing, a most depressing and unpleasant sight.

Mites on a leaf.

This is where your careful inspections and notes about your plants will pay off. You are much more likely to notice the very beginning of a spider mite infestation because you will have trained yourself to observe every detail of the plants' appearance. It is far better for the plants and your eventual harvest success if you spot the initial infestation and act quickly before it gets out of control. If you wait until your plants are covered with spider mite webbing, it is probably too late to save the plants.

What to Do If You Have Mites

Spider mites thrive in dryish conditions, approximately 20–30 percent humidity. They also crave warmth. In temperatures above 80°F, spider mites can reproduce themselves in as little as five days. The indoor cannabis grower has to walk a fine line between humidity levels that are unattractive to spider mites and the higher humidity desired by destructive molds that also plague cannabis, like botrytis or powdery mildew.

During the vegetative stage of cannabis growth, periodic blasts with a forceful jet of water can physically remove and kill many mites, as well as destroy the webbing. It is thought that spider mites may delay egg laying until new webbing is produced.

Treatment in an Isolation Ward

The very first preventative is to make certain you do not unknowingly bring infested plants in contact with your grow room or any cannabis plant, whether indoor or outdoor. Spider mites can live on plants other than cannabis, so any plants you handle or purchase should be inspected for spider mites, not just your cannabis.

Since the initial indications of spider mites are so tiny, it is possible that, with all good will in the world, another grower provides infested clones, perhaps at a compassion club event. Never put these new clones or plants in with your existing crop without a period of isolation where you can inspect them closely under magnification and give a preventative bath with an organic insecticidal soap. The insecticidal soap kills the spider mites by compromising their cellular integrity, and the spider mites are dissolved from the inside out.

Observe the new plants for at least a week, checking carefully under magnification for any sign of spider mites. If they pass as clean, give them one more treatment with the organic insecticidal bath, and transfer the plants out of isolation.

↓ LOW-CO$T TIP

Make your own insecticidal soap with two to three drops of a soft, biodegradable soap (like Murphy Oil Soap, Castille, or Ivory liquid soap) per quart of water. Apply the bath by using a clean spray mister bottle, or with small clones, simply dip them into a wide-mouthed jar of the solution. If you are dealing with larger plants, make certain to cover every inch of the leaf, especially the undersides where spider mites prefer to live. You may have to repeat this every other day; the soap only stays effective for about a day.

If you find a really nasty infestation but still want to salvage the plants, you can use something a little stronger. Some growers recommend spraying plants with a 1:1 mixture of alcohol and water to kill spider mites on contact. Rubbing alcohol evaporates quickly and should do little damage to the plant, though it is advisable to test the spray on a few leaves first and check the plant's reaction. Other growers prefer a 1:3 mixture of rubbing alcohol to water to make the spray gentler to the plants. As with the soap solution, make sure to cover the entire plant, especially the undersides of the leaves.

Another alternative is horticultural oil, like neem oil, an extract from the neem tree. This is an excellent alternative to nonorganic compounds for controlling spider mites.

HASSLE-FREE TIP

Neem oil should always be used in strengths recommended by the supplier; doubling up on the amount of oil may injure your plants. Neem oil should be applied during the day to ensure quicker evaporation, which will reduce your chances of damaging the plants. Plants that are noticeably under water stress should not be sprayed with oils.

If you find spider mites on new plants or clones, you should realize that you are now a vector that can carry the spider mites along to your healthy crop. The best thing is to treat the infested plants, remove all your clothing and bag it for removal to a washing machine, and immediately shower or bathe yourself.

Although all of the above may seem like a lot of trouble, it is nothing compared to what you are faced with if you get spider mites established in your grow rooms.

Organic Solutions

Some growers think that chemical solutions to the spider mite problem are acceptable to use as long as they are used early on in the vegetative phase of the cannabis grow. Putting aside the human health implications of using chemicals on a consumable, the grower needs to understand spider mite control and not just blindly spray poisons.

Very few insecticides are effective for killing spider mites. Chemical control of spider mites generally involves pesticides that are specifically developed for spider mite control: miticides or acaricides. Because most miticides do not affect the spider mite eggs, a repeat application at ten- to fourteen-day intervals is needed for control of hatching eggs. Frequent applications of miticides help create resistant strains of spider mites, making their control even more troublesome.

Natural Enemies

Natural, and extremely effective, enemies of spider mites include small lady beetles, predatory mites, minute pirate bugs, big-eyed bugs, and predatory thrips. Spider mites, especially in an outdoor grow, usually only become problems when the use of insecticides destroy their natural enemies.

For example, carbaryl, commercially known as Sevin, devastates most spider mite natural enemies and can greatly contribute to spider mite outbreaks. Malathion, despite being advertised frequently as effective for mite control, can actually aggravate spider mite problems instead of preventing them. Systemic, or soil-applied insecticides like Marathon or Merit, both of which contain the chemical imidacloprid, have also caused spider mite outbreaks by eradicating all their natural predators.

Spider mites have many natural enemies that limit their numbers in gardens, especially when unharmed by pesticide sprays, but the most useful ones are mites in the Phytoseiidae family, which are predators of spider mites. In addition to naturally occurring predatory mites, some are produced commercially for release as biological controls.

HASSLE-FREE TIP

The predatory mites most frequently available by mail order are *Galendromus occidentalis*, *Phytoseiulus persimilis*, *Mesoseiulus longipes*, and *Neoseiulus californicus*. These are quite successful in controlling spider mites in indoor cannabis grows; predatory mites often like the higher humidity of a cannabis grow room, which is helpful as spider mites do not tolerate humidity very well.

The predatory mite *Phytoseiulus persimilis* cleans up after itself. Once the spider mite population is gone, they feed on each other, decimating their own populations.

Metaseiulus occidentalis is another common predatory mite used to kill spider mites. It is an effective biological control only if temperatures are on average between 44°F and 89°F.

Phytoseiulus longipes is a variant of the *Phytoseiulus persimilis* mite brought in from Africa. It can stand warmer ambient temperatures than its North American cousins. *P. longipes* has quickly become the most popular biological spider mite control agent used by gardeners.

Most suppliers provide information regarding use of the predator mites that they carry, but as a general rule of thumb, predatory mites should be placed out at a count of at least twenty per plant. The predators have difficulty moving from plant to plant, so they need to be placed on each individual plant. You can place more if you like, depending on the state of your spider mite infestation. It is estimated that one predator mite can eat twenty spider mite eggs or five adult spider mites per day. Like many super-specialized biological controls, most of these predators will die once the food source (in this instance the spider mite colony) is fully depleted.

For information on where to buy these predators, write or call California Department of Pesticide Regulation, 1101 I Street, P.O. Box 4015, Sacramento, CA 95812-4015, (916) 324-4100, and ask for a free copy of their leaflet "Suppliers of Beneficial Organisms in North America," or view the leaflet online at *www.cdpr.ca.gov/docs/ipminov/bensuppl.htm*.

Other insects feed on spider mites and provide high levels of natural control. One group of small, dark-colored lady beetles (also called ladybugs), *Stethorus* species, are known as the spider mite destroyers; they are extremely specialized predators of spider mites. Additionally, minute pirate bugs, big-eyed bugs (*Geocoris* species), and predatory thrips are important natural enemies that can help the outdoor cannabis grower should you accidently bring spider mites to your grow site.

Other Prevention Techniques

Another nontoxic weapon in the battle against spider mites is the use of sticky traps. You can create them by smearing a sticky resin like Tanglefoot on pot edges or cardboard that is an attractant color like yellow. Some indoor growers have had success with this trapping strategy: smear cardboard panels with Tanglefoot, being careful not to touch it, or the plants, with your hands. As your fans rotate, the spider mites are blown off and stick on the Tanglefoot panel. You can also put Tanglefoot around air intakes to trap incoming spider mites looking for a home. Of course, you will still need to treat the plants for spider mite eggs, but reducing the adult population will help you gain control.

Spider mites prefer dry conditions (one reason they are so prevalent in the more arid areas of the United States), so properly managing the moisture level of your plants is critical to prevent an outbreak. Plants stressed by lack of water also produce changes in their chemistry that make them more nutritious to spider mites. Spider mites also feed more under dry conditions, as the lower humidity allows them to evaporate excess water they excrete.

The indoor grower of cannabis has more control over how humid the grow environment is kept and should provide an environment that is less hospitable to spider mites. Overall, the best treatment is extreme caution, close observation of the plants and the grow environment, and prevention before infestation.

CHAPTER TWELVE

DEALING WITH MOLD

Next to cannabis thieves, almost nothing else is as detrimental to a crop as molds. Different types attack at the new seedling stage (damp-off), some at the vegetative stage (the powdery type mildews), others at full flowering (gray mold, or botrytis), and, of course, the cannabis stays vulnerable during the hanging, curing, and storage phases of production. The wise grower maximizes his chances of a bountiful harvest if he follows some simple steps to prevent molds.

What Is Mold?

Healthy plants require the presence of beneficial fungi and bacteria; however, there are some pernicious versions of both that are massively destructive to your goal of successfully raising and harvesting high quality cannabis. One of the worst molds to attack cannabis is botrytis, a pathogenic fungus also commonly known as gray mold or sometimes blight. Botrytis is found virtually everywhere plants grow and attacks many different types, not just cannabis and hemp.

This observation is not meant to be discouraging but to emphasize how vigilant you must be in observing your plants and the need to take immediate steps to prevent and/or eradicate botrytis. As a small grower, you will have the ability to monitor all your plants very closely and provide individualized care for each of them.

How Does Mold Start Growing?

Botrytis, the most destructive mold to cannabis, must have high humidity conditions (50 percent or higher) and nutrients or some food source before it invades the plant. This is why good garden practices are important. Any debris from old leaves or bruised, broken plant parts can be enough to provide a food base. This mold is frequently found in greenhouses or indoor grow rooms, though rainy conditions near harvest can provide perfect conditions for a botrytis outbreak in outdoor crops. If ignored and left unchecked, eventually the fungus will invade healthy plant tissue, and you will lose a significant portion of, or even all, your harvest.

To help prevent infection, monitor each plant on a daily basis for the following problems, and remove or repair:

- Fallen leaves, at base of plant, or hanging on axials
- Injured leaves
- Broken stems
- Cuttings from botrytis infected plants
- Wounded tissue where cuttings were taken

Botrytis is spread by the wind or in water, or on your hands or clothing. Almost any activity can result in a release of spores and subsequent transfer to the crop. Botrytis initially forms two types of resting structures on or in infected plant tissue. The fungus then waits for the right high-humidity condition to erupt into destruction mode.

What Does Mold Look Like?

Botrytis appears sometimes within hours of a plant inspection. The reason for the common name of gray mold becomes apparent when you first see the gray, smokelike eruptions of spores appear on the flowers of your prized plants. Unfortunately, the mold starts from within the flower, so your first indication of botrytis can be only the tip of the iceberg. The mold can initially be mistaken for a dusting of trichomes, but once in full bloom it presents as gray, almost hairlike, spots on the cola or flower, continuing rapidly to a slimy, dark gray mess.

Botrytis starting on a flower. (Notice the mold spot.)

Full blown botrytis.

Mold Prevention While Growing Cannabis

Sanitation and good air circulation are the best weapons the grower has to prevent major botrytis or other mold outbreaks. Remove dead leaves or damaged tissue from the plants and keep the garden area extremely clean. Do not throw dead leaves to the base of your plants; you are only creating a food source for botrytis and other molds. If you have plant breakage or cut tissues (from accident, high winds, or taking cuttings for propagation), repair immediately.

You will note that cannabis stalks and stems appear hollow inside. Water can collect where the plant has been injured or cut and provide a nice damp spot for mold to start. It is worth your while to seek out some pure beeswax (for the best price, check online for local beekeepers to buy from, or you can purchase at health food stores or candle making shops).

Remove any darkened or bruised looking plant tissue with a clean, sharp knife or pruning shears, warm the beeswax in your hands to soften, and make a little plug. The warmed wax will be pliable and easy to shape. Smooth the top into a little cap so that all cut plant tissue is covered with wax. Some growers use chewing gum for the same purpose, but beeswax, due to its purity and waterproof properties, is preferred. Be sure to thoroughly clean your knife or shears in between cuts. Otherwise, you could be spreading what you are trying to prevent. Dip shears in a solution of one part bleach to four parts water.

Outdoor growers must rely on existing weather and humidity conditions over which they have no control. Initially planting for good air circulation and constant monitoring of the crop for beginning outbreaks will go a long way in determining how much of your harvest can or will be damaged by mold. Bushier plants, and very thick, dense colas need to be gently inspected on a daily, and preferably twice daily, basis. Part the branches (be gentle to avoid breaking) and examine the inner parts of the plant; the center of dense vegetative growth receives the least air circulation.

Once you spot botrytis, you must react immediately. If you have outdoor plants, and they are near finish, remove any infected parts, bag in plastic, and then harvest the plant. Shower and change your clothes after handling infected plants; never go directly from handling botrytis to a clean plant, or you will spread the spores.

Powdery Mildew and Downy Mildew

Both these mildews present in a similar manner, and the treatments are virtually the same. Affected leaves typically display blotchy spots in yellow or bronze and an overlying white, powdery fungal growth. These mildews are favored by high humidity but not necessarily free water on leaves. Warm temperatures and shady conditions encourage the fungus to grow and spread. Luckily, the spores and mycelium (vegetative part of the fungus) are sensitive to extreme heat and direct sunlight.

The optimum temperature for infection is between 68°F and 77°F, and relative humidity between 40 and 100 percent is sufficient for the spores to germinate. Low, diffuse light also seems to favor powdery mildew development.

In general, healthy, vigorous leaves and stems are less prone to infection. Plants under nutritional stress, in most cases, will develop mildews much sooner than plants the same age grown under a good nutritional program.

Outdoors, make sure plants are not crowded and are in full sunlight and in a well-drained area. Indoors, use dehumidifiers and maintain good air circulation and ventilation. Ideally, always water your crop in the morning.

Another organic option is to spray once a week with a solution of baking soda. Do not spray more often than once per week, as added frequency may add too much sodium, something your plants will resent. Baking soda increases the surface pH, making it more alkaline and unsuitable for the growth of mildew spores. Spray the undersides of leaves as well as the upper surfaces when using any sprays.

Baking Soda Spray
- 1 tablespoon baking soda
- 1 gallon water (alkaline water with a pH of just below 8 is best)
- A few drops of liquid soap (to help the solution stick)

Neem oil (available at garden stores) is an organic solution for both molds and mites. Always use sparingly and follow directions; more is not always better and can be harmful.

Damp-Off or Pythium Wilt

Damp-off, in which the little taproot becomes infected with a fungus parasite and rots, is primarily a problem with young seedlings. Start out with sterilized soil, avoid heavy watering, and provide adequate ventilation. If your previously vigorous little seed starts to suddenly lose momentum, there's a good chance you are over watering. Also be sure to check the humidity levels and for adequate air circulation.

Mold Prevention While Drying

While your harvested crop is hanging, drying, and curing, you must continue with close inspections on a twice-daily basis, especially if you brought the plants in due to onset of mold. Keep the humidity level as low as possible. If need be, purchase a dehumidifier and, of course, maintain constant gentle air circulation.

How to Check Drying Plants for Mold

Under good light, examine each plant from top to bottom. You will have already removed the fan leaves (see Chapter 13), so check each cola for any signs of mold. Remove any cola that shows mold and dispose of carefully. Clean your tools and hands, and change clothes after handling moldy plant materials. This reduces the danger of spreading spores to clean plants.

At-risk plants (those with very dense, bushy colas) may need to be taken apart wet and dried in parts. The thicker colas may show no sign of mold until you expose the inner parts of the flowers. Some indica crosses can have massive central top colas that are very prone to mold. Botrytis in particular starts growing within the flower, so the onset is hard to spot.

Sometimes a plant needs to be removed from the drying area and broken up for salvage. It depends on how far gone the mold outbreak is, and the act of breaking apart the colas can spread spores. If you have thick, dense colas and see botrytis outbreaks all over the hanging plant, the odds are good that the insides of the colas are going to look scary. Do not hesitate to take all the colas apart and be ruthless in deciding what to dispose of. There is no "sort-of okay" area. If it is moldy, get rid of it!

Mold Prevention During Storage

Once your crop has finished hanging and drying, you will manicure the flowers for storage and store them for the longer curing process. Manicuring the flowers allows for close scrutiny of each individual flower for mold. Make certain you have good bright light to work under; sometimes in dim light, a dusting of mold can look like trichomes. You do not want to store moldy flowers with clean ones.

Some growers use an interim step of storing the manicured flowers in brown paper grocery bags. The paper breathes well. The flowers should be gently stirred every one to two days. Or you can go straight to plastic zip-top bags or, preferably, glass jars with sealable tops (like Mason jars). Whether you use bags or glass, make certain to breathe the cannabis by unsealing and resealing once per week. Smell the cannabis as you unseal it; you will notice the difference as soon as the plant material stops gassing.

Mark your calendar for breathing, and stay on schedule for the next six to eight weeks of curing; otherwise, you will ruin your harvest. Molds need moisture, so, as with any herb, store your cannabis in a cool, dark, dry place.

CHAPTER THIRTEEN
PROPER CURING AND STORAGE OF YOUR HARVEST

Harvest is a very exciting time of year, especially on the outdoor grower's annual cycle. The indoor grower has the option of several harvests throughout the year and can look forward to safely curing, storing, and sampling each one. How you handle the plants now will have great effect on the quality of the harvest. Inattention can result in molds, overdrying, or improper curing that can destroy the aroma and taste. For many health and aesthetic reasons, moldy cannabis should never be used.

Preparing Plants for Curing

There are a few different thoughts on how to properly hang cannabis for curing. Some growers prefer to hang the entire plant. This requires a fair amount of height in your drying shed, as well as more space in between plants. Since the first-time grower is unlikely to possess an empty barn, you'll probably cut your first crop into branches and dry them in sections. Some growers even take each individual cola and hang them to dry, but, due to space requirements, this is only advisable with small harvests.

Plants almost ready to harvest.

Start prepping your drying area well before harvest time. Not being ready takes a lot of the fun out of the process, and being disorganized can cause you to lose track of which plants are which, especially if you cut the plants into branches for hanging.

You will need:

- Heavy-duty eye bolts
- Heavy-gauge wire (size 17 gauge or larger)
- Wire cutters
- Step ladder
- Drill
- Screwdriver
- Paper grocery bags
- Electricity
- Multiple oscillating fans
- Good light

Setting up your drying shed will require a little visualization and measuring. You will be amazed at how large the plants appear to become when you bring them indoors. This is just the visual contrast created by enclosing them. This volume will only last a few days; much of it is water contained in the plants, plus you will be trimming the remaining fan leaves as you hang the plants. Bear in mind that you most likely will be bringing the outdoor plants in a few at a time as each individual plant should be harvested as near to peak maturity as possible.

Note that proper drying requires a cool, dry place with no direct sunlight. If there are windows in your shed, make sure to cover them with curtains or shutters. A good overhead electric light is important so that you can closely examine the plants daily for mold, but direct sunlight will degrade the quality of your harvest.

Depending on genetics and placement in the garden, different plants will be ready to harvest within a few weeks of each other. This gradual harvesting is helpful as you will have plants that have been hanging and drying and already using less space. These can be moved closer to each other as the newly harvested, bulkier plants come in.

Preparing Your Drying Space

To prepare your drying shed, first make certain the cobwebs and other dust and debris have been vacuumed out with a shop vac or vigorous work with a broom. Wash the flooring and make the shed as clean as possible. You may occasionally drop a branch or even an entire plant, and avoiding contamination and dirt are the name of the game.

You will be placing your eyebolts to support long runs of the taut hanging wires. Do not try to use heavy-duty fishing line or rope; these will bow in the middle of your run and cause the hanging plants to slide together. Until the plants shed their water weight, the hanging lines will be supporting an enormous weight.

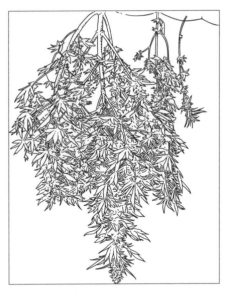

Preparing the plants for hanging.

Because an average axial branch can easily reach five to six feet in length, estimate the height needed to have the branch tips clear your floor by at least a foot—two feet is better. This is where your stepladder comes into play; you will need it for setup and for attending to the hanging plants. Of course, if your shed has more length than height available, it is perfectly fine to cut the longer branches in half and to hang them lower.

HASSLE-FREE TIP

Always hang plants or branches top down. Never hang with the roots still attached; retaining the roots will not help the quality of the harvest and may add dirt to your flowers.

Allow enough space to move in between the rows, as you will be checking the plants for mold from all angles at least once per day, as well as continuing to trim fan leaves.

Airflow Requirements

As soon as your first plant comes into the drying shed, begin using the oscillating

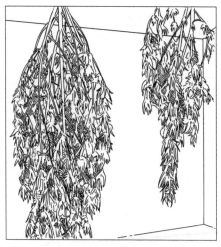

Hanging plants.

fans. The fans should be placed to maximize airflow around the hanging plants while avoiding a direct blast continually blowing on them. Avoid having the fans positioned too low as they may blow up dust from the shed floor. As the wet plants come in, set the fans on high; as the plants dry out more, lower the fan settings to maintain a gentle continual cycling of air.

Ideally you will have harvested outdoor plants under clear skies, but frequently plants are brought in based on the weather and the ongoing forecast. If it has been raining for a week and the plants are close to or completely finished, you will most likely bring them in to dry. The chance of a few extra days of finishing is offset by the threat of mold.

As noted above, wet plants are very, very heavy. Before bringing them into the drying shed, give the plant a good shaking to shed as much external moisture as possible. New growers should not worry about shaking the newly harvested plants; the resins are super-sticky and cannot be shaken off at this stage.

If the plants are truly rain soaked, be prepared to cut the plants in pieces for hanging. At this time you will start stripping the fan leaves that remain; this will help reduce weight and keep the large, wet fan leaves from touching the flowers and inducing mold. The big paper grocery bags on your list are for these leaves. Removing the fan leaves also makes it much easier to quickly check the flowers for molding; otherwise, you will need to lift leaves to examine the flowers.

Drying Fan Leaves

Many growers do not bother with fan leaves; in part this depends on the size of the harvest. If your harvest is small, you will want to use every part of the plants. The fan leaves can be useful for producing bubble hash.

Bear in mind that law enforcement views large fan leaves as cannabis and will count them for weight should they try to enforce some sort of legal limit or prosecute you for growing cannabis. So stay tidy, keep track, and either process to hash, destroy, or donate the leaves to someone who can use them immediately.

If you plan on using the leaves, stir the bags daily to help them dry. Otherwise, remove the bags as they fill up and destroy the fan leaves. This will speed drying, as the fan leaves will not be releasing additional moisture into the air of the drying shed. You can either feed them to goats (they love cannabis leaves) or burn them. Composting the leaves is not advised, as, again, these can be seized by law enforcement as supposedly useable cannabis.

The Importance of Good Handling Practices

Always bear in mind that you are producing a product that will be ingested by humans, either by smoking or eating the cannabis. Particularly for medical cannabis patients (whose health is often greatly impaired), cannabis should never be allowed to mold. Even with the best practices, hanging cannabis is very, very vulnerable to molds and great care must be taken to identify and remove problem spots immediately.

↓ LOW-CO$T TIP
Molds can greatly reduce your harvest's yield; it is not uncommon to have a pound and a half of superb bud reduced to a few salvaged ounces or completely destroyed within forty-eight hours. As with most of the other stages of cannabis production, vigilance by the grower is imperative for a successful harvest outcome.

When and How to Take Clippings

There are many variables to consider when determining how long to hang your harvest: weather, moisture levels, plant size and type. Expect a minimum of two weeks hanging, with a good possibility that you will wait six to eight. The easiest way to tell if your cannabis is ready to clip is to check smaller branches for "snap." A branch that is gently bent between two hands should break, not bend. It does not have to snap in half (this would be too dry), but there should be a definite break. Again, as with harvest, the plants will be ready to clip at different times, so each plant must be checked individually for finish.

Clipping Tools

Preparing to clip means having the right space and tools. Clipping a large crop is fun, but it can be a laborious process. You want to have a big table and chairs at a comfortable height for long periods of sitting and working with your hands. You need good light so you can examine the buds closely as you clip. Common sense dictates that the clipping room is not exposed to casual visitors, either by viewing through porch windows or folks stopping by to visit. You will need:

- A pair of pruning shears
- Large sheets of clean glass (framed picture glass is good)
- A pair of small sharp scissors for each clipper
- Gallon zip-top bags
- A Sharpie or other indelible pen
- Large brown paper grocery bags

It's best to clip one plant entirely before starting another because there's less chance of mislabeling product. Besides, the way the plants are hanging make this a logical progression as you work your way through the drying shed.

Allow approximately one hour to clip one ounce. This is only a general rule of thumb; some plants' structural characteristics make them an "easy clipper." Other types have lots of extraneous sugar leaf and require more finicky scissor work.

If you estimate a general yield of a pound per outdoor plant, just one plant is going to take approximately sixteen hours to clip.

Multiply that by your plant numbers and you should have a fairly good estimate of how much time to plan for clipping activities.

The Clipping Process

Now that your clipping table is set up, you are ready to go. Decide on your first plant and pick up your pruning shears. Cut enough axial branches to make a nice bundle; your table size will dictate how much to start with. Place a paper grocery bag to the left and right of each chair; one will be for bigger remaining fan leaves, and the other for the sugar leaf. You might as well separate the two at this point, as excessive handling can knock the crystals off the dried sugar leaf.

As you work on the plants, keep an eye out for your marked "seeder" branch(es), unless you have already put the seeder branches in a separate area for drying. These should be set aside for careful examination during a seed session.

Start stripping fan leaves off the larger branches; you can do this with your hands. This is advisable, as your fingers are going to get very tired of feeling scissors (blisters are common when clipping big harvests). Cut the smaller branches off the bigger axial and place over your glass (the glass will catch large amounts of kief which can be made into the delightful finger hash).

Take your scissors and cut the colas off the branch, right at the nodes. When you finish the branch, you have the option of trimming another one and stockpiling colas to fine clip, or fine clipping as you go. Each person clipping will find a rhythm and process that fits his style; there is no single correct way.

As you fine clip the colas, the goal is to remove the small sugar leaves. Keep moving the sugar leaves to one side of your glass and the finished colas to the other. Periodically put the sugar leaf into your other grocery bag.

Storage

When your pile of colas is big enough, label a bag with the plant's information and set them in zip-top bags. Depending on the flower characteristics (fluffy or dense), a gallon bag should comfortably hold a quarter pound of colas. You do not want to pack the bags tightly, as you want to avoid crushing and packing down the flowers. If your harvest is small, clean, dry Mason jars are wonderful for storage but require a great deal more space than the plastic bags.

"Breathing" Stored Cannabis

As your cannabis flowers hang and dry, they will end up at about 25 percent of their fresh weight. At this point they are dry enough to store, but they will continue to cure. Drying and curing cannabis actually takes a fairly long time. Depending on the amount of humidity in the drying room, just drying hanging cannabis can take up to eight weeks. Curing continues as the chlorophylls and other pigments in the flowers start to break down. This is what will remove the "green" taste that is associated with uncured cannabis.

Never seal your dried harvest into plastic or glass without periodically breathing the containers during this curing period. This will release gases that the plant matter continues to release. If you fail to vent these gases, the bad taste is trapped and you will end up with some fairly nasty tasting cannabis.

Many growers find it helpful to mark their calendars, breathe the bags or jars once a week, and continue to sample the plant. Usually the curing process takes two to four months, so keep evaluating for progress. You will also notice that when you open a sealed container it no longer puts forth a rush of chlorophyll smell but the sweet aroma of properly cured cannabis. Once curing is completed, you can seal your containers until you want to use the cannabis. Never freeze cannabis; this will have harmful effects to the resins you worked so hard to produce. Store your cannabis in a cool, dark place.

Common Problems and Solutions

The biggest problem outdoor growers hope to experience is suddenly realizing that they have far more green plant material to hang up than they had planned for. This can be dealt with, as the plants are going to lose a lot of water weight and bulk very quickly. Sometimes a spare room has to be put into use for a day or two, but do not panic; you will be able to move the hanging plants quite a bit closer to each other very soon. A shower rail can make an excellent temporary hanging spot for a large plant, or even the top rails of a canopy bed. You can use these temporary spots while you continue to clip off fan leaves, which will also quickly make the plants less bulky.

Another common problem is finding animal hair stuck to the flower resins. This most frequently happens during the drying phase when cats or other household pets are allowed in the drying room. Always make certain the room has been well vacuumed before hanging your plants, and keep your pets outside.

Sometimes you will discover mold issues beginning as you are preparing plants to dry; this is fairly common and just requires a few days of close attention to air circulation and the removal of any mold outbreaks immediately. Always wash your hands and any cutting tools in alcohol and be very careful to not spread mold from plant to plant. Larger colas may need to be taken apart. If they are extremely dense and have a lot of moisture content, you want to increase the air circulation immediately or risk losing a lot of good flowers to mold.

Do not run heaters to try to speed drying; drying too fast will ruin the taste and texture of the flowers. Cannabis needs a cool, dry, dimly lighted, and low-humidity environment to dry at the proper rate. Direct sunlight can bleach and dry plant material too quickly and again affect the quality of your end result.

HASSLE-FREE TIP

Sometimes trying to hang entire plants just does not work. Either the height of your space is less than optimal, or the plants themselves have branches that fold together and inhibit air circulation. It is perfectly fine to cut the plants apart; just make certain that you keep the branches labeled.

Most problems with drying and curing can be avoided by paying close attention to the plants, checking for mold at least twice a day, adjusting the fans to assure even air circulation, and keeping temperatures cool. If your drying room is in your home, you will have to either not turn on your heat or make certain that the drying room remains unheated until the plants are finished hanging. Once the plants are safely manicured and placed into containers, always remember to breathe the bags regularly, and you will end up with well-dried and cured cannabis.

CHAPTER FOURTEEN

RECORDKEEPING

There are many benefits to keeping accurate records of your cannabis grow, and some significant risks as well. While licensed medical growers in medical cannabis states can keep their records without fear, the illegal propagator in other states should remember that these records can and will be used as evidence by law enforcement in any criminal proceeding. For that reason, you should not keep your records on your computer, and it's best to devise a coded system. Do not leave your grow records out lying around; keep them locked up as with anything of value.

Why Keep Records?

If you are growing cannabis for the first time, and only for yourself, you might well ask "Why keep records at all?" There are several reasons.

Growing, and growing well, even with a few plants, is a continual learning experience. Because there are many steps involved, having a system to complete and record the steps decreases the chance that you will overlook some. And, if you grow once a year, it is especially easy to forget details of parentage, start dates, temperature variations—any of the minutiae of the garden.

If you keep detailed notes, you are training yourself to note things like temperature and humidity levels, what day is the last frost day for your area, if plants are always smaller in a certain area of your grow site, and where the sun moves to during the outdoor cycle. These are just a few of the things that will help you understand your plants and their performance.

If you are a medical cannabis grower, recordkeeping becomes even more important. You need to monitor which strains work for which patients and note the feedback the patients give you on new hybrids or strains. This is different from recreational use because it is not whether your customers like the cannabis but whether a particular strain alleviated their symptoms. If you have patients who have trouble articulating their experience, it is helpful to know how to ask the right questions.

If you are a seed breeder, detailed records are essential; otherwise, you are breeding blind. You can breed without notes or records, of course, but instead it can leave you not knowing how you produced something spectacular and searching, perhaps in vain, to reproduce it.

And last but not least, records of your expenses are very helpful, especially when you can be reimbursed for them. People who have never grown cannabis, or gardened in any way at all, have a naive idea that growing outdoors is "free." They forget about water bills, fencing costs, minerals, soils, alarm systems, and other expenses of a serious garden.

What to Record

The first entries for your grow book should include whatever information you have about the seed or clones you are using to start your grow. This could be a detailed profile of a certified strain you purchased or were lucky enough to have given to you. It's also very possible that you are not sure what you have, but you might have more information than you initially think. Sources can be as nebulous as "Pete says really good smoke, he bought it in Portland and found some seeds." You will know if Pete's appraisal is based on recreational or medical effects. You also will be able to estimate the quality knowing what he thinks is really good smoke, another nugget of info. This information, though not ideal, is actually a reasonable beginning for the profile you will build about each plant you propagate.

In general, you want to record the source for your genetics, whether seed or clones; the dates of propagation, breeding, harvesting, curing, clipping; success or failure of breedings; final product weights; descriptions of product performance; and a daily log of temperature, feedings, waterings, and transplantings by date.

When to Record

Pete has told you all he knows about the origin of the seeds under discussion. It is still worth writing down this information. The purchase in Portland makes it a good guess it was grown on the West Coast, most likely in Oregon. The seeds found in the finished product would indicate most likely outdoor grown and therefore vulnerable to random, wind-borne pollination. The geographic location would give a strong chance that the seeds are from an indica hybrid; these are more viable than pure sativa types in northern Oregon's shortish outdoor growing season.

Your initial note on this plant profile would still be "Pete says really good smoke, he bought it in Portland and found some seeds," but you might add "possibly indica" and put the date you received the seed. If Pete can remember, put the date he found the seed. This will give you some approximation of the seed's age. If, for example, you got the seed in 2006 and are trying to germinate it in 2010, you would know that less of the seed is likely to germinate (having passed the three-year optimum mark), and soak more seeds from the beginning. Then you would note how many actually germinate and how soon.

HASSLE-FREE TIP

Divide your grow book into two parts. The first part is a daily garden journal where you note temperature, humidity, general activities like scheduled feedings (how much and what), and waterings or rainfall if outdoors. The second part records information about individual strains or plants and includes notes about the general appearance and performance of the plants.

Once you have seedlings, you will note their type of leaf formation and whether it is typical of a sativa or an indica. Until your seedlings sex, you should group them under an easy to remember name that also gives information, like Pete's Portland Pot. The strain source, should Pete's recommendation prove to be true and you end up propagating and creating a strain from his seeds, will always be "PPP 2006."

Creating Strain Profiles

An important part of your grow book will be a profile of each strain group. If you are using clones, you will have the same name for each plant of an identified strain as they are genetically identical. Some growers number each plant within the strain group—for example, White Widow 1, White Widow 2—and track their individual performance that way. This will give you valuable information about which spots are best in your outdoor grow or perhaps areas in your indoor growrooms that need adjustment to the lighting or ventilation. The plants are going to act with variation, and your notes will help you figure out why.

Hybrids and Naming Plants

If you have bred from seed and created hybrids, the best way to keep track is to name each individual plant. Each is unique, unlike the clones. Ideally their names will reflect what you know about the origins. If we go back to Pete's seeds, let's say you have germinated and raised ten seedlings to the point of sexing. You now have six females and four males. If you want the pollen, pick the strongest, healthiest male and isolate him. There is no need to name him; he is still PPP, but the year changes to the current grows. Therefore, "PPP Male 2010" is sufficient for knowing your pollen source. The other males can be destroyed. You will note in your book that they were terminated as opposed to being casualties.

Now you have six females. The easiest thing to do is give them all "P" names, so, for example, you would end up with Petra, Penelope, Persephone, Paulette, Primrose, and Prunella. Each generation from these females can be named in a way that gives you an easy way to recall their genetics even without looking at your notes. Plants designated by numbers are much harder to recall.

Think of it this way: if a few years down the road you have a plant named "Whippersnapper," it would be far easier to remember that her mother was "Prunewhip," whose mother was "Prunella," whose source seed was Pete's Portland Pot, than to remember a sequence of numbers. Of course, you will have your grow book for reference, so the system you use is really more a matter of personal preference.

How to Record

As discussed above, your grow book will have two sections, three if you are growing for medical as well as recreational users. The medical section will record which strains are for what symptoms as you receive feedback from the patients.

The Daily Log

The first section will be a daily log of all your activities with the plants, from procuring clones or starting seeds, weather conditions, feedings, and so forth. This can be written like a journal and provides a record of that particular grow. Even though your plants will be labeled, it is helpful to make a placement map of each plant, depending upon the size of your grow. Obviously if you only have three plants, you will know exactly which plant is where.

Some samples of this sort of entry would be:

- 4/15: Received three (3) White Widow clones. 4" in height, healthy. Dipped and in isolation.
- 6/10: Transplanted (6) Nancy B. Green X Sparkle Toes to 2 gallons. Light rain. 71°F.
- 7/23: NBG X ST starting to sex. (2) females so far. 86°F. Watered all.
- 9/26: Starting to rain. Too muggy out. 76°F. Watch for mold. Nancy Toes brought in this morning, checked for mold, and hung in big drying shed. Started fans today.

Mostly you will keep a daily journal, but the examples are to show how simple and brief the information can be. The weather and temperature information is very valuable to the outdoor grower; you will be able to see patterns for your particular microclimate and to plan your grow's scheduling more accurately each successive year. Of course, every year will have some variations, but keeping these sorts of notes will help you notice indicators that will eventually help explain differences in the plants' behaviors.

Strain and Plant Profiles

The second section of your grow journal will be a profile of each strain, and if growing from seed, each plant itself. Note as much of the genetic information as you can, the date the seed tailed, the date of planting, the date the seedling came up, characteristics of the phenotype, dates bred and to which male, the date harvested, date clipped, final product weight, and performance evaluations (such as whether it lived up to its potential or exceeded it). Note some details about the taste, aroma, and psychoactive effect. If you bred the plant, note the appearance and number of seeds produced by the breeding.

If you grow for patients, it is important to keep a profile for each patient and which strains work for their illnesses. Ask your patients to rate each strain as to taste and aroma, as medicine should be palatable. Cannabis is so complex that effects can be very specific depending on the properties of the specific strain. Ask detailed questions as to the timing of onset of pain or nausea relief, or relief of a specific symptom such as muscle spasm. Have them rate the symptom relief on a scale of 1 to 10. Ask how long the effect lasts. Some strains will not relieve some symptoms at all, so these are important questions to have answered; you want to find the best possible strains for your patients.

The other thing to be aware of is that some strains may relieve symptoms but will cause the patient to be very drowsy. These are useful for sleep, but listen to your patients' feedback; they also need strains that provide for symptom relief but let the patient stay alert and functional, called daytime strains. Typically these will be some sort of indica/sativa hybrid. Eventually you will be able to provide your patients with a good range of medicine that helps them to manage their symptoms, but it takes a dialogue and some experimentation. Taking good notes will help you to identify what works for which patient a lot faster.

↓ LOW-CO$T TIP

A good old-fashioned hardbound blank book works very well for recordkeeping and can be carried around the grow with you as you make your notes. It is generally not a good idea to keep these records on your computer. Laptops can end up damaged by water or dirt if you try to carry them around in the grow environment.

At the end of the day, the simple recording of your plants' life cycle will make you a much better grower. The more you note, the more you notice, and you will be training your eye to spot problems well before they are out of control. The outdoor grower will become much more able to evaluate plant sites and place plants for the best growth; the indoor grower will notice nuances of grow room performance that lead to more productive light placements or better feeding schedules. The plants will benefit greatly and will thank you by being beautiful, healthy, and productive.

CHAPTER FIFTEEN

TROUBLESHOOTING

Every gardener or grower of cannabis will have times when the plants are puzzling and things are not going right. First you will notice that something seems a bit off. You suspect, you worry, you watch, and then finally you have confirmation that you have a problem. All growers go through these troubled times. Some garden problems, like rippers or hailstorms, can be unexpected and devastating to the crop's success, but most plant problems can be prevented by focus, foresight, and proper gardening practices.

Plants Are Yellow

Seedlings and young plants in the vegetative phase should not have yellow leaves. The leaves should be a uniformly deep, healthy green. Yellowing can indicate a variety of different problems. Your first response should be to test your soil for pH levels and for N-P-K. Plants that are nitrogen starved will yellow, starting with the older leaves and continuing until the entire plant has yellowed. Cannabis uses nitrogen for stem and leaf growth; a nitrogen-starved plant will grow slowly and appear stunted.

Sometimes novice growers think if some is good, than more is better. Not so! Excessive fertilizing can burn the plants and cause yellowing as well.

Testing the pH is essential. If the soil is too acid or too alkaline, the plant will not be able to use the soil's available nutrients. If the soil's pH range is not between 6.5 and 7.5, the plant's food is locked up. Blindly adding more nitrogen to acidic soil will just compound the plant's problem, so it is very important to test the pH first.

Magnesium, manganese, sulfur, and boron deficiencies can all cause some type of yellowing. A magnesium deficiency shows initially in older leaf growth, while a lack of sulfur shows yellowing in the newer growth. Starting out with a well-balanced organic soil is the best preventative.

Yellowing leaves from nutritional problems should not be confused with the plant's natural cycle. As cannabis proceeds into and through the peak floral stage, the outer leaves will yellow, wilt, and drop. This is perfectly natural; the amount of yellowing and leaf drop depends, in part, on the genetics and phenotype of each plant. During the peak floral phase, avoid propagating mold by cleaning up dropped leaves and grooming the plants to remove loose, yellowed leaves on a daily basis.

Also note that cuttings that are in the process of rooting will show some yellowing at approximately one week, especially on the lower leaves. This is normal and will rectify itself once the root system has developed.

Plants Are Not Growing

There can be a number of reasons for stunted plant growth: poor soil, poor drainage, lack of nutrients, lack of light, temperatures too hot or too cold, and excessive humidity or dryness. Other reasons may be fungal root infections or pest infestations.

Poor performance by seedlings is an indication of damp-off; you have used contaminated soil or the growing medium is too wet. Gently dig up the most pitiful specimen and inspect its root; damp-off thins the plump white root in sections. Generally you will have to start more seed, using clean soil and sterilized pots. Make sure not to overwater young seedlings and inadvertently create a welcoming environment for damp-off. Provide good air circulation and ventilation at all times.

Seedlings will also grow slowly if their environment is too cold. If you grow outdoors, make certain you are not trying to get too far ahead of your local growing season. If you want to get seedlings started early, you must provide enough light and warmth indoors, and plan for a period of hardening off when you transfer the plants outdoors.

Cannabis growth is very rapid during the vegetative phase. If your plants are not transplanted to larger containers or fed for growth in smaller containers, they will eventually run out of room and food.

HASSLE-FREE TIP

As always, a quick check of pH and N-P-K levels will give you a great deal of information, and probably point you to the correction needed.

Next to unhealthy pH levels, bad drainage is probably the most common cause of stunted growth in cannabis. Cannabis hates soggy soil and responds by sulking and growing slowly. Conversely, cannabis also has big water requirements and drinks deeply. If you consistently forget to water your plants, expect poor growth performance.

If you are growing outdoors in the ground, and just one or two plants suddenly slow dramatically, look carefully around the grow site for telltale gopher mounds. Gophers throw up soil from their tunnels and can appear quite suddenly in outdoor gardens, partly because your good soil is full of earthworms and other food they find tasty. You do not have to see the gophers, and probably will not. The mounds will let you know they have invaded.

Unfortunately, a gopher will power right through a cannabis root ball, severely impeding the plant's support system. If you plant directly into the ground, you should line the planting holes with chicken wire. Once you realize you have gophers and your plants are already in the ground, there is no moving the plants without causing great stress and shock to the plants.

Green Leaves but No Flowers

This could be caused by a number of reasons. The indoor grower must trigger flowering by cutting the light cycle to twelve hours. If the plants still make no move to begin flowering, check that the dark phase is truly dark. Light leakage can confuse plants. The outdoor grower must wait until the sun's cycle reaches this critical trigger point for cannabis. Make note of how many hours of sun the plants still receive, and check for light sources outdoors that may be disturbing the plants. Certain genotypes will flower later than others. Many outdoor cannabis breeders place a lot of emphasis on strains that flower early, particularly in areas that typically have heavy fall rains.

Check the N-P-K ratio of your plant's food. You may be feeding too much nitrogen during the flowering phase. The plant needs lots of nitrogen, approximately 10-7-8 during the vegetative phase, but continuing to feed too much will delay flowering after the light changes. Flush the soil with plain water, and feed flowering plants more phosphorus, using a 4-8-8 ratio. Plants should be allowed to become nitrogen deficient late in flowering; some growers say this improves flavor.

Plants Are Wilting

Sometimes plants become overheated, or their soil has dried out. The obvious solution is to give them water, and water deeply so the plant gets a good drink. The plants should become turgid again very quickly.

Sometimes, however, the problem can be damage to roots or salt buildup in soil. Not much can be done after roots are damaged, but flushing the soil with clean water can help leach out excess salts.

Mold

Different types of molds and mildews attack cannabis at all phases of growth and production. If unidentified and left unchecked, eventually you will lose a significant portion of, or even all, your harvest. Generally, when cannabis growers say they have mold, they mean they have an outbreak of the dreaded botrytis.

Botrytis, or gray mold, is the most destructive to cannabis. It requires high humidity conditions (50 percent or higher) and debris from old leaves or bruised, broken plant parts to provide a food base before it invades the plant. Rainy conditions outdoors, high humidity indoors, and the natural leaf drop near harvest time can provide perfect conditions for a botrytis outbreak. To prevent infection, remove dead leaves or damaged tissue from the plants, and keep the garden area clean as well. If you break a plant accidentally or take cuttings for propagation, repair immediately. Once you spot botrytis, remove any infected portion immediately, adjust humidity levels, and monitor each plant on a daily basis for continued outbreaks.

Once the plants are hanging, make certain to check humidity levels and to provide excellent air circulation. Examine the plants carefully twice a day and remove any spots of mold as soon as they appear. Some growers take a lighter or barbecue starter and burn the area where they have removed botrytis. This may have the effect of completely drying out the wet, mold-infected area and preventing further spread on the plant.

Mites

Spider mites reproduce rapidly in the hot conditions of a cannabis grow room. Plants under water stress are highly susceptible, so make certain to water on schedule.

Spider mites are so tiny that an initial infestation is easy to miss until you start seeing damage to the plants. Examine your plants closely with a handheld lens with at least ten times magnification. Spider mite eggs are usually laid near the veins of leaves during the growing season; they look like little drops of water until they become cream colored just before hatching. Check all over, but particularly on the undersides of leaves for old hatched eggshells as well as the adult spider mites, their eggs, and the distinctive spider mite webbing.

Adult spider mites have eight legs and an oval body, with two red eyespots near the head end of the body. The immature spider mites resemble the adults, except the newly hatched larvae have only six legs.

Spider mite colonies can contain hundreds of individual mites and produce very distinctive silk webbing on infested leaves. The presence of this webbing is the easiest way to distinguish them from other types of mites. Lightly misting your plants before inspecting them will make the webs much easier to see. If you spot mites, act quickly and bathe the plants with an organic insecticidal soap, or use organic neem oil. Make certain to get the undersides of the leaves and the entire plant; leaving any spider mites behind will just start the cycle all over again.

Other than seeing the spider mites themselves, the first signs of an infestation show up as a scattering of light-colored spots on the plant's leaves. As the infestation continues, the leaves take on a sickly gray or bronze color, eventually turning yellow and dropping off. The entire plant can become engulfed in spider mite webbing. At that point, destroy the plants and clean and sterilize your grow rooms.

HASSLE-FREE TIP

Always check new plants from outside sources very carefully for spider mites. If the plants were started indoors, be especially wary. Keep the new additions isolated from your other plants until you are certain they are not carrying spider mites. This little bit of extra care will pay off over and over.

Deer

Deer eating cannabis is primarily a rural grower's problem, but not always. Outdoor growers in more urban areas know that deer are quite apt to move around at night, particularly in cities with large parks.

The rural grower has more trouble if he lives in a drought-prone area. All that well-watered, green, delicious cannabis looks worth a lot of risk to a hungry deer. They will jump very high if they need food. The grower in this area needs to use at least ten-foot fencing—twelve is better and safer.

A grower who lives in a green belt should be less concerned. If you have rose bushes, the deer will prefer them, particularly after the cannabis starts heavily producing resins. A lower fence, even six feet, will suffice. Rural deer do not like to jump into anything that could trap them if they have other food choices. It is only during droughts that they get desperate and take risks to eat fenced-in cannabis plants.

Urban deer in drought areas will frequently wander into enclosed areas. Urban deer are much less afraid of people because no one can shoot at them. Rural deer are spookier; they know that humans have guns and that they frequently use them.

Some growers save dog hair from clipping their dogs or get some from a dog-groomer friend. They put it in the brush around an unfenced grow to discourage deer. Another deterrent that sometimes works is sprinkling blood meal around the site.

LOW-CO$T TIP

To discourage deer, wind string around in the brush. Again, the deer will not like how traplike the string appears and feels.

Tarps or old metal roofing panels laid on the ground around the crop site will discourage deer as well as elk or sheep. The texture and sound make them unwilling to walk across either of these. Just bear in mind that goats have no trouble walking across almost anything, so do not confuse goats with sheep.

Gophers

Many types of burrowing rodents can take up residence in a garden. Gophers, pocket gophers, moles, and voles are some of the more common ones. Usually you will notice gophers because their tunnel digging creates mounds of fresh earth. These appear very suddenly and are quite large.

Gophers can be quite destructive to plants that are ground planted. They are not really after your cannabis, but they will tunnel right through an unprotected root ball if it appears in their way. The best solution is to line your planting holes with chicken wire, leaving a standing rim of wire at least eight inches in height. This will keep the gophers from making the planting a point of entry, and the lower wire protects the plant's root ball. The exposed chicken wire will also alert you to remove it should you later till the planting area.

Moles tunnel along just under the surface and are usually not harmful to cannabis plants, unless they get into a large raised bed and cannot figure out how to get out again. The chicken wire gopher solution will work fine for moles, too.

Voles are small rodents, and they sometimes girdle a cannabis plant's trunk by gnawing away the bark and the cambium around the plant's trunk or main stalk. This kills the plant by interrupting the circulation of water and nutrients. Protect the stalk with chicken wire.

All of these rodents can be eradicated by a good garden cat. Make certain you get a cat of proven hunting ability, as not all cats are good hunters. Some growers use gopher traps. These can be effective, but always make sure to cover the set trap with a heavy bucket so other animals like pets do not get hurt. Never use poisons.

Wood Rats

If you grow in a wooded area, you and your plants may have an encounter with wood rats (genus *Neotoma*). These are also known as pack rats or trade rats, and are about the size of the common Norway rat. They have a furry tail; soft, fine fur; large ears; and light-colored feet and bellies.

The first indication you will have of wood rats is that some of your cannabis will be missing branches. Then some more branches will be missing. Wood rats are mostly active at night and feed primarily on green vegetation, twigs, and shoots. Most species of the wood rat family build a large stick den or house on the ground or in trees. Some of these houses are as big as four feet in size. A nest, usually made of finely shredded plant material, is located within the larger house.

First, locate their stick house nest. This is usually fairly easy as the structures are so large. It will not be too far away from your crop site. You will find your cannabis branches neatly woven into the structure. Then, sadly for the wood rats, you must destroy the nest. Sometimes this is sufficient to make the wood rats move on to more friendly territory. Sometimes it's not.

One grower reported success by setting their cannabis containers inside moated circles. The wood rats that tried to cross the water all drowned, probably because they could not climb out of the slippery plastic sides of the moats. Some growers scatter mothballs around the base of their plants. This has varied success and is not advised due to the chemical nature of mothballs.

If you must kill them, wood rats are easily trapped with standard rat-sized snap traps. Good baits include peanut butter and dried fruits. As with using any trap, cover or secure it so children or other animals cannot get hurt. Always wear gloves when emptying a trap, as wood rats are a vector for plague and other less-than-enjoyable diseases.

Broken Branches

Although cannabis is usually very strong, on some occasions a branch will break, either from accident, high winds, or the weight of the colas pulling it down, and it tears from the trunk. If this happens, just take the branch in and hang it to dry and use. Fill the wound left on the trunk with some beeswax. Lower branches that are pulling away can be propped with five-gallon plastic buckets laid on their sides. The weight of the branch holds it in place, and the bucket supports the too-heavy branch. Higher branches can be propped or tied, but this generally has limited success. You can try to see if the plant responds, but it is generally better to cut and treat with beeswax.

Corn Earworms

Some growers have never had to deal with these little pests; some growers have had episodes and then did not see them again for years. They actually seem more common in outdoor urban grows, perhaps because backyard corn growers are sometimes untidy gardeners and create a habitat for corn earworm moths and their caterpillars. These are small, smooth-skinned, little green caterpillars, generally with a thin white horizontal racing stripe. Their coloration is a perfect camouflage for hiding on cannabis; the green is sativa-green, and the thin white stripe looks like a cannabis flower pistil.

The corn earworms love to bore into cannabis buds, just as much as they love to bore into the tips of growing ears of corn (hence their name). Sometimes, the first indication a grower has that corn earworms are eating the crop is to actually see an apparently healthy large cola drop from the plant to the ground. Cannabis flowers are very firmly attached to the plant; something has to eat through the stem to remove a flower.

A corn earworm is more likely to be seen where corn has been growing. An initial infestation starts because a corn earworm moth lays eggs in the soil. These hatch into the little green caterpillars that eat your cannabis, then drop back into the soil to pupate and become the moth that will then lay the eggs and so on in an elegant cycle.

As soon as you spot the earworms, pop them with your fingers and leave their little corpses on a larger older leaf of the plant. Go over and groom every inch of your plants at least twice a day, handpicking the earworms. The earworms do not seem to attack the leaves of the plants particularly. They treat the cola, or flower, like an ear of tender young corn. Since leaves are starting to die back as the plants produce flowers, you will be grooming the plants every day at this point anyway. Pay more attention to the colas if you have spotted earworms; remember, they like to burrow to the inside of the flower.

If you notice earworms right before harvest or at harvest, you will be able to perform a night capture of most of the earworms left on each plant. Hang the harvested plants as you normally do, and put some light-colored tarping underneath. Periodically check, but within a few hours in the dark, the earworms start to let down from the plant, each on a long, silver individual thread. Somehow changes in the plant's chemistry tell them the plant is dying (it has been cut down) and they need to get to the ground to pupate so they can return as the moth in the spring. This is your chance, and you must be ruthless about killing them all.

If you grow a well-balanced and organic garden with your cannabis interspersed, you will find that beneficial insects and birds are tremendously helpful. If you do find yourself with an earworm outbreak, birds are your cannabis's best friend.

Earwigs

Earwigs are generally not a problem after your cannabis grows beyond the seedling stage. They can snip off very young seedlings, however, so be careful when you put seedlings outside to harden off. Make sure the area is clean of debris; earwigs hide under bark or in old plant pots or any sort of dark hiding place convenient to the plants.

A good earwig trap can be made by rolling up newspaper or using short lengths of small PVC pipe. Take a bucket of hot sudsy water with you and tap the traps into the bucket every morning.

↓ LOW-CO$T TIP
You can protect your seedlings during this phase by placing clean jars over the little seedlings at night. This is a little time-consuming, depending on the size of your grow, but only needs to be done for a week at most. After that the seedlings will get too big to be bothered by earwigs and your traps will have done their work.

Pill Bugs

Pill bugs are actually crustaceans. They are known for their ability to roll into a ball and are sometimes called roly-polies. They are most active at night and are only really hazardous to cannabis during the small seedling stage of the plants. A very special treat for pill bugs are monocotyledonous leaves, which are the first little leaves a seedling opens. Protect your seedlings from pill bugs as you would against earwigs; as soon as the plants are at least eight inches tall, the pill bugs will leave them alone. Pill bugs are generally useful in compost piles where they help break down dead plants and eat different fungi.

Aphids

Sometimes cannabis can be attacked by aphids, a sucking insect that stings the plants. As aphids feed, they also exude a honeydew or sugary sap. The honeydew attracts ants and can also make a good environment for black sooty mold. Aphids also spread disease from sick plants to healthy plants as they feed and migrate back and forth. The best solution is to wash the aphids off the plants and buy some ladybugs. Ladybugs come in bulk through mail order, and most garden centers carry them as well.

Slugs and Snails

Both slugs and snails can cut down seedlings and shred leaves of older plants. Protect your seedlings as you would for earwigs, and get rid of the pests by handpicking and destroying. This is best achieved at night when they come out to feed on your plants. Drop the slugs and/or snails into a bucket of soapy water as you pick them. A dusting of diatomaceous earth around main plant stems is a good way to keep them from getting to larger plants. Diatomaceous earth is made from fossils of freshwater organisms that have been crushed to a fine powder. The powder particles resemble bits of broken glass when observed thru a microscope and are very destructive to slugs and almost any insect while harmless to humans and animals. Diatomaceous earth can be found at almost any garden center.

Thrips

Thrips are small, flying, plant-sucking insects that are generally most damaging in greenhouses. Thrips are becoming a problem in soilless greenhouses that use rockwool and hydroponics. In old soil-floored greenhouses, a soil fungus could grow that infected and killed thrips when they dropped to the ground to pupate. Soilless growhouses have no damp soil and fungus for biocontrol. Use sticky traps to catch them on the wing, and apply insecticidal soap spray until you get them under control.

APPENDIX

GLOSSARY OF TERMS

acclimatize
The physiological adaptation of a plant to changes in climate or environment, such as light, temperature, or altitude.

acidic soil
Soil with a pH value below 7.0.

aerate
Loosening packed soil to allow water and air to penetrate.

alkaline soil
Soil with a pH value above 7.0.

asexual propagation
Directed reproduction of genetically identical plants, accomplished by taking cuttings.

ballast
Regulates electrical flow; used in indoor grow systems.

blood meal
Organic fertilizer containing high nitrogen; made from dried blood from slaughterhouses.

breathing
Opening stored dried cannabis to release chlorophylls. Term used in the cannabis curing process.

bud
Slang term for a cannabis flower.

calyx

A small pod containing the male or female reproductive organs in cannabis.

chromosome

Any of the organized components of each cell that carry the plant's individual hereditary material, or DNA.

clipping

Manicuring or removing the leaves from dried cannabis flowers.

clone

A rooted cutting from a plant, or as a verb, the asexual propagation of a plant.

cola

Slang word used for the cannabis flower.

cold frame

Unheated glass or plastic greenhouse for protection of young plants.

compost

Fully decomposed organic matter. High in valuable bacterias and nitrogen.

cotyledons

The rounded seed leaves that first appear on a plant.

crossing

Creating a hybrid by breeding two unrelated individuals.

curing
A slow process where cannabis becomes more palatable and dry enough to store without breathing the containers.

cutting
A slip taken from a parent plant for asexual propagation by cloning.

damp-off
A damp-loving fungus that attacks young seedlings' initial roots, and young clones' stems. Also known as wire-stem or pythium wilt.

dioecious
Sexually distinct; the male and female reproductive organs occur on different individual plants. Cannabis is dioecious.

drill
A seed-planting hole, usually made by a premeasured stick.

fan leaves
The largest leaves on cannabis; primarily light gatherers.

fertilization
To unite male pollen with the female plant ovary.

fungus
An organism of the Fungi kingdom. Mold, mushrooms, and mildew are fungi.

gene pool
Assembly of all gene combinations available in a population.

genotype

The specific genetic makeup of an individual plant; a combination of genes inherited from the parent plants that is unique.

germination

The seed sprouting process.

hardening off

The process of gradually acclimating greenhouse plants to the outdoors.

hashish

A strong pyschoactive made from the compressed resins of the cannabis plant.

hemp

Very fibrous, low-THC cannabis. Used for making textiles and fuel.

hermaphrodite

A cannabis plant with flowers of both sexes appearing.

hybrid

Offspring resulting from crossbreeding two different gene pools.

indica

Short for *Cannabis indica*, a species of cannabis, particularly found in medical cannabis strains.

leach
Washing or flushing soil of soluble components, achieved by heavy watering.

leafing
Also known as grooming; removing yellowing or dead leaves from flowering plants.

marijuana
A common term for cannabis.

mildew
A powdery mold found on leaves.

mother plant
A female cannabis plant used as a source for clones by taking cuttings.

mulch
Surface dressing, preferrably with compost, to reduce water evaporation and to provide plant nutrients.

N-P-K
Nitrogen (N), phosphorus (P), and potassium (K); essential elements for plant life.

organic gardening
Gardening by natural method; without synthetic chemicals.

phenotype
The expression, or outward, form of a plant, created by how the environment influences the genotype.

photoperiod
Duration of daily exposure to light, whether artificial or natural sunlight.

photosynthesis
The process in green plants by which carbohydrates are synthesized from carbon dioxide and water using light as an energy source. Plants then release oxygen as a byproduct.

pistils
Fuzzy white hairs that appear at the tip of the female calyx in pairs. Used to catch male pollen.

pollen
Microspores that contain the male plant genes.

pollination
Transfer of male pollen to the female ovules for seed production.

primordia
The earliest stage of both male and female cannabis flowers that first appear along the main stalk and limbs.

root ball
The plant's roots and the soil contained by them.

root bound

A condition where a plant's roots have filled its container.

sativa

Short for *Cannibis sativa*, a species of cannabis known for its strong psychoactive effect. Frequently crossed with the indica species.

senescence

A natural phase of decline in a plant; from peak to death.

sexual propagation

Reproducing plants by fertilization.

shake

Slang term for lower-grade cannabis, meaning mostly leaves.

sinsemilla

A Spanish word meaning "without seeds," commonly used slang for the preferred state of recreational cannabis for consumption.

soilless medium

A mix made of vermiculite, perlite, sand, and pumice that is sterile and contains no nutrients.

sport

An individual or new genetic character arising or resulting from mutation.

stamen

The pollen-producing reproductive organ of a flower.

sticky traps
Any number of organic pest solutions that involve a nontoxic, nondrying sticky substance spread on attractant colored sheets of cardboard.

strain
A line of offspring from shared ancestors.

terpene
A hydrocarbon found in resinous plants like cannabis or rosemary; the organic molecule of strong aroma.

tetrahydrocannibinol (THC)
One of the psychoactive chemicals found in cannabis.

transplanting
The process of transferring plants to larger containers or into the ground.

trichome
A plant hair that secretes resin.

vegetative phase
The growth phase of cannabis preceding the flowering phase.

vermiculite
A soilless medium used by indoor growers for moisture retention.

INDEX

DAILY BENDER

Want Some More?

Hit up our humor blog, The Daily Bender, to get your fill of all things funny—be it subversive, odd, offbeat, or just plain mean. The Bender editors are there to get you through the day and on your way to happy hour. Whether we're linking to the latest video that made us laugh or calling out (or bullshit on) whatever's happening, we've got what you need for a good laugh.

If you like our book, you'll love our blog. (And if you hated it, "man up" and tell us why.) Visit The Daily Bender for a shot of humor that'll serve you until the bartender can.

Sign up for our newsletter at
www.adamsmedia.com/blog/humor
and download our Top Ten Maxims No Man Should Live Without.